SPECIAL MESSAGE TO READERS

This book is published under the auspices of

THE ULVERSCROFT FOUNDATION

(registered charity No. 264873 UK)

Established in 1972 to provide funds for research, diagnosis and treatment of eye diseases. Examples of contributions made are: —

A new Children's Assessment Unit at Moorfield's Hospital, London.

•

Twin operating theatres at the Western Ophthalmic Hospital, London.

•

A Chair of Ophthalmology at the University of Leicester.

•

The establishment of a Royal Australian College of Ophthalmologists "Fellowship".

You can help further the work of the Foundation by making a donation or leaving a legacy. Every contribution, no matter how small, is received with gratitude. Please write for details to:

**THE ULVERSCROFT FOUNDATION,
The Green, Bradgate Road, Anstey,
Leicester LE7 7FU, England.
Telephone: (0116) 236 4325**

**In Australia write to:
THE ULVERSCROFT FOUNDATION,
c/o The Royal Australian College of
Ophthalmologists,
27, Commonwealth Street, Sydney,
N.S.W. 2010.**

I've travelled the world twice over,
Met the famous: saints and sinners,
Poets and artists, kings and queens,
Old stars and hopeful beginners,
I've been where no-one's been before,
Learned secrets from writers and cooks
All with one library ticket
To the wonderful world of books.

© JANICE JAMES.

NEVER TOO LATE

The author's third book of memories, MANY FINGERS IN THE PIE, relates the rapid changes that took place in farming after World War II. There were, of course, also changes in the author's own life as her five children were born. The book closes with the death of her beloved husband, Sid, nine weeks after they had left the farm in the capable hands of their son, Michael, and retired to a bungalow.

NEVER TOO LATE, is the author's account of her life after her husband's death. She also writes about her children and grandchildren, and of her trips abroad. She travelled on her own several times to Canada to visit her son, David, spent a month in Kenya and fulfilled a life-long ambition to cruise on the Q.E.2.

Books by Ellen Smith
in the Ulverscroft Large Print Series:

MEMORIES OF A COUNTRY GIRLHOOD

ELLEN SMITH

NEVER
TOO LATE

Complete and Unabridged

ULVERSCROFT
Leicester

'Many Fingers in the Pie'
First published 1985

'Never Too Late'
First published 1986

First Large Print Edition
published 1996

British Library CIP Data

Smith, Ellen, *1907* -
    Never too late.—Large print ed.—
    Ulverscroft large print series: non-fiction
    1. Wymeswold (Leicestershire)—
    Social life and customs
    I. Title
    942.5'47

    ISBN 0–7089–3562–1

Published by
F. A. Thorpe (Publishing) Ltd.
Anstey, Leicestershire
Set by Words & Graphics Ltd.
Anstey, Leicestershire
Printed and bound in Great Britain by
T. J. Press (Padstow) Ltd., Padstow, Cornwall

This book is printed on acid-free paper

MANY FINGERS
IN THE PIE

To my children John Sidney,
David Warner, Michael William
and twins, Richard Gordon and
Elizabeth Helen

Foreword

My third book of memories relate the rapid changes that took place after World War II. In the space of a decade tractors displaced horses, combine harvesters saved the labour of several men, and electric dryers did the work that used to be left to the sun. Electricity came to our village in 1933, and when main water was piped in a few years later, many modern machines were installed, easing the work-load. Silage took the place of mangolds and turnips, saving many hours of backbreaking work.

During this time many important events took place in our personal lives. We at last had the daughter we had wanted for so long. She had a hard time surviving her birth, and her twin brother fell dangerously ill shortly afterwards, but both recovered and we took great joy in seeing them grow up.

Our son Sidney was fortunate enough to take over the tenancy of another farm. Shortly afterwards, all the farms in the village were put up for sale by Trinity College, Cambridge, and we helped organize the farmers into a group to purchase the land we rented.

I shall also tell about our poultry ventures, including the change from free-range to controlled environment; about the Women's Institute which started in our village in 1933; and finally about the restoration of our village church, under the guidance of an energetic young vicar.

Once again I should like to thank all who have helped and encouraged me in the production of my books: there have been so many fingers in the pie. I should also like to thank here the hundreds of readers who have phoned or written their appreciation of my stories. They are far too numerous for me to answer them all individually. I feel greatly moved when I read them and I shall treasure them all my life.

Wymeswold, 31 May 1985

1

New Developments on the Farm

MY husband Sid and I had worked very hard at our farm at Wysall Lane End, Wymeswold. With our three sons, John Sidney, David Warner, and young Michael William, we hoped to make many improvements in the years following the declaration of peace. During the war the government had controlled the prices of most farm products, paying a very fair price all round. This had enabled farmers to plough back into the land more than they had been able to do for years. Like many others, we took advantage of this piece of luck. We more than tripled the number of our poultry, reared more calves, and instead of two breeding sows, we had quite a number of gilts to establish a good young herd of pigs. We also put a bit of money in the bank with which to pay for the expected

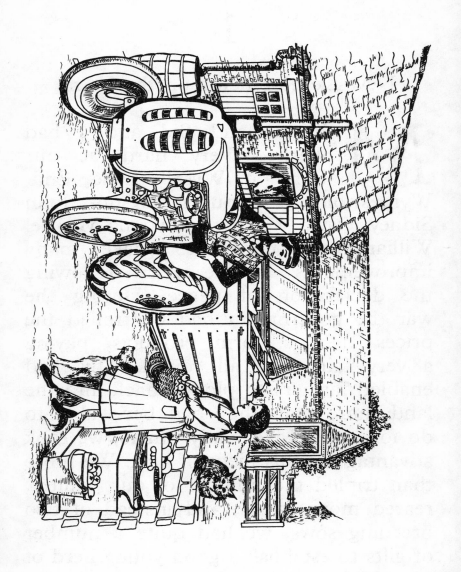

improvements. Sid and I believed in the old way of life as regards spending money: we never bought anything unless we had the money to pay for it. I think the old saying that expectation is sometimes better than realization might be true: I always enjoyed saving for something specific. Nowadays things are just the opposite: buy first, pay later.

After the war ended, farming started to alter in many ways. For example, machines gradually took the place of horses. When Michael was around four years old, we bought our first tractor, a second-hand Ford Standard which had huge iron wheels on the front and rubber tyres on the back which could be changed for iron spade lugs. After a few years these iron wheels were banned because of the damage they caused to the roads by making deep marks on the tarmac, but they were still allowed to work the land. This was alright for farmers with land that surrounded the farm-house, but with farms like ours where one had to travel over a mile by road to some of the outlying fields, this seemed a major financial blow. These old tractors had no self-starters, and always had to be started with a handle. On a cold winter's morning this could be real hard work, and many men suffered sprained wrists when difficult engines refused to start. Michael remembers driving this old tractor in the fields by the time he was six years old. These days one would not be allowed to let a child that age even sit on a tractor, as it is a punishable offence until a child is 13 years old. Michael loved driving: he used to sit in the front seat of the car watching his father manipulating the gears, so that before he was eleven years old he could drive our old car in the fields.

The first major development on our farm was a new cow-shed to house ten cows. It was to cost £300 and to be built on a site we called the wood-pile, but which was really a dump where everything unusable was put out of the way. Trinity College, Cambridge, the owners of the farm, agreed to finance this project but required a rent adjustment. We started to clear the site in readiness for my Wootton brothers, the local builders, to dig the foundations. This cowshed was the first job they had obtained since the war, during which all local building had been terminated and they had taken jobs with the Air Ministry. When peace came, they wondered if work would be difficult to obtain, but after building this cowshed they went from strength to strength, eventually building many private houses in the village as well as an estate called Trinity Crescent for the Barrow Rural District Council.

We had great fun clearing the site, finding a number of things that had been lost for years, including Sid's first set of false teeth, which must have been thrown out with the rubbish. Sid had a habit of taking out his teeth — to rest his mouth, he said — leaving them in impossible places. He was always asking me: "Nell, have you seen my teeth?" Once I found them on the shaft of a farm cart. Another time they were found sitting on a wall outside our house. This last time they were lost for a few years, and were found in a heap of old plaster. They were quite clean, but I disinfected them, then Sid put them into his mouth and they fitted perfectly.

With the addition of ten cows to our herd, making much extra work, our thoughts turned to the idea of a new tractor, with a front fork-lift loader which would help the moving of manure. We finally bought a Massey-Ferguson tractor and a new trailer to go with it. The tractor cost just over £400, the trailer £70. We certainly found the benefit of these new machines, but at the side of the huge tractors of today, they were tiny but very efficient. Gradually we bought the necessary accessories — a plough, harrows and equipment for the production of potatoes. We had never grown potatoes in the fields before, we just grew enough in the garden for our own use. During potato-picking time we all turned out to help and the children would bring their friends who earned quite a bit of money. As we enlarged our acreage of potatoes, we employed women helpers. Sidney used to take the Land Rover to collect them at various points, then take them home after a day's work. Sid used to space out the ground, to be fair to each worker, but some women were always grumbling that they had more to do than some of the others. Now, if possible, Sid liked to employ local labour at these times, but he got so tired of the women grumbling that one year he engaged a gang of Irishmen who were very hard workers. In our early potato-growing years, we always stored them in the fields in what were called clamps. The potatoes would be stacked about five feet high and around ten feet wide, then they would be covered in straw, then soil, leaving an air-space at the top. In extreme winters a lot of potatoes would get frozen, and then turn bad. These days they are generally stored inside, surrounded with bales of straw.

With all these new machines, the man who drove them still had to work in all weathers without cover of any kind. Nowadays a cab to a tractor is compulsory. Although we were thrilled with these new implements, we were sad to see our heavy horses becoming redundant. We kept most of them until we found good homes for them. Daisy, our oldest mare, was sold for very little money to a smallholder who was too old himself to convert to new machines. We were so pleased to find someone who needed a horse for just light duties. We could have made much more money if we had sold Daisy for meat, which was so popular on the continent, but we had owned her right from a foal, and hated the idea of her going across the Channel in an overcrowded boat, only to be slaughtered at the end of it. We kept Blossom, who was Daisy's daughter, for many years. The younger, stronger horses were sold, but we kept our Welsh pony, Bob, until he died one extremely hot summer.

Many horses died that year. The extremely hot weather dried up the grass, forcing them to eat off the hedgerows where deadly nightshade flourished. One evening as I watched Bob being taken out to pasture by our young farm-helper, I noticed he walked as though he was dreadfully tired. I knew he had not been overworked that day, as all he had done was to trot about three miles morning and evening for the milking. (During the summer months we milked the cows in a small shed in the fields.) This unusual lethargy in such a spirited horse worried

12

me all the evening, so when Sid came home, I begged him to go to the field just to make sure the pony was alright. "Oh, you worry too much, Nell," he grumbled. "It is because of this extreme heat." Nevertheless he went, just to ease my mind. Sid thought the horse was alright, so I cast off my worry, went to bed, and I enjoyed a good night's sleep. But the next morning Bob was so ill we sent for the vet, who told us the pony had deadly nightshade poisoning and had only a fifty-fifty chance of recovery. We had to make him drink the gruel I was to make while the medicine the vet gave him had time to work. I stayed with that wonderful, lovable horse for three days and two nights, most of that time with his head resting across my tummy, where he seemed to be most comfortable. He gallantly drank all of the gruel I gave him until the third day when he was much too ill to try any more. By this third day I knew he was losing the battle, and the poison was taking its toll. His legs were swollen to double their normal size, then his testicles swelled enormously. He became weaker and started to stagger.

I held his head lovingly against my tummy, but at last that great spirited horse collapsed and died. I felt drained after all those hours without sleep, and I sobbed continually for several days. My family were wonderful during Bob's illness: they looked after themselves, and had only bread and cheese for dinner each day. But oh how we missed our beloved horse! At the age of sixteen I had helped break him in, and he had never put a foot wrong. In fact, my brother Warner said he broke himself in. Never before or since have I loved a horse as much as I loved him.

With ten more cows added to our herd of sixteen we needed more grass land, so when a twelve-acre field just outside our village went up for auction, we thought we would try to buy it. I waited at home full of anxiety on the night of the sale. I could not go with Sid, as we had a new cow calving at that time and someone had to stay behind in case of need. The cow had a lovely calf, but I lost it because I left a piece of mucus over its nose and mouth which killed it by suffocation. Sid arrived home with the wonderful news that we had bought the field for just over £800. We were sorry about losing the calf, but were much too excited about buying our first bit of land to be unduly worried.

Our next labour-saving device was a milking machine. To install this meant having a new building to hold the machine, sterilizing equipment, and a cooler for the milk. During these improvements main water was piped to our village, which enabled us to have water pipes and bowls fitted in all our outbuildings. This saved a tremendous amount of work carrying water to our animals, and for all household purposes. (Our well water had been condemned.) And oh! The magic of turning on a tap!

We then thought about turning a small back bedroom into a bathroom. What a boon that would be, a cosy bathroom, instead of bathing in the outside wash-house in the summer, and in front of the living room fire in the winter. We wrote to Trinity College, Cambridge, offering to pay half of the cost of installation, if they would pay the other half. To our great surprise this offer was accepted and the work was to start immediately. Usually when we requested any improvement, there were many consultations and delays, and the rent was slightly raised. In a matter of weeks our lovely new bathroom was finished, with a Marley tiled floor, and white tiles around the bath. This was luxury indeed, with a hot-water tank, and a large airing-cupboard. All of our family enjoyed this easy way of bathing, without the hard work of preparing and clearing away the water.

A thing which puzzled us for a long time was the fact that the Trinity representative brought along two men from the Council to examine our new bathroom. It was not for many months that we learned of the help the local councils were giving to owners of houses who put in new bathrooms. We then realized why our landlords were so quick to consent to these improvements. We paid half the cost, the Council paid the other half, which meant that Trinity College had improved its property without spending a penny! A slick piece of business I would think. When the councils started giving this help, the public was slow in learning about it, but these days everyone seems to know.

Now we had electricity and water on our farm, both Sid and I had a little more leisure time, so we were able to take time to ourselves, while my unmarried sister Lottie looked after the children. Sid was extremely fond of attending horse-race meetings. He took me to Ascot one year where I saw most of the royal family. Being a dressmaker myself, I really enjoyed seeing the wonderful fashions of the day. It was an experience I have never forgotten. We both enjoyed many other race-meetings, going to Newmarket, Epsom, Doncaster, Lincoln and, of course, our own Leicester, Nottingham and Melton Mowbray.

The Quorn Hunt races at Melton were much enjoyed by many of the local farmers and their families: they were considered a special day's outing once a year. When I was a child, I remember my father telling us of the splendid meal the farmers enjoyed at the Quorn Hunt's expense. Each farmer who had allowed the hunt over their fields was given tickets for the races and the dinner, but during our own years of farming only tickets to enter the race-meeting were given and the dinner was discontinued. The Quorn Hunt, however, is still generous to farmers who suffer broken fences and damage to crops. If foxes kill poultry, the farmers are even recompensed for their losses, although during the last decade very few hens are kept on free range, almost all being kept in battery-houses.

Sid studied form to his great advantage. I did not bet myself, and really did not like Sid betting quite so much, but he promised me very solemnly that his betting would never hurt me or our family. In fact, he gave much of his winnings to charity. One night he came home and emptied his pockets. His winnings, when counted, amounted to nearly forty pounds, which was an awful lot of money at that time. I gasped: "Have you really won all that money tonight, Sid?" He assured me he had. The thought entered my head that forty pounds would enable us to start the Wymeswold teenagers dancing again. I mentioned this to Sid, and he asked me to explain. "Well," I said, "forty pounds would buy a very good powerful record-player, and enough dance records to make a start." Sid and I had always loved dancing, and wanted our children to learn, too. Sid gave me every penny of his night's winnings, but advised me to get someone to go with me to buy the record-player who knew something about them, as I knew nothing. The next morning, which was a Saturday, a friend and I travelled to Loughborough and bought the record-player and around twenty records.

We advertised by putting posters around the village saying we would be starting village hops the next Friday and every Friday through the winter. We had a marvellous response because during the war years the young ones in our village had been starved of recreation. Often seventy or eighty girls and boys would attend. Sid and I did our best to teach them the basic steps of dancing. It was very hard work, but as time went on, other older people who liked dancing joined us, and this was a great help.

We learned that quite a number of

the youngsters wanted to learn old-time dancing. Sid and I took this request very seriously, so we went every week to the Unity Hall at Sileby where they had an old-time dancing club. We enjoyed learning these dances, along with new sequence dances. By the end of winter, our kids, as we called them, were enjoying both modern and old-time dancing, with a few dances that were called party-dances. This gave Sid and myself great satisfaction. Years and years afterwards, when these teenagers had children of their own, they used to thank us for enabling them to learn to dance.

I chuckle when I remember an incident that happened one night while we were taking an old-time course at Loughborough College. Sid needed to leave the room, but he was such a long time away I began to worry. The toilets were outside, so I took a walk to see if I could find out the reason for this very long absence. No one was in sight, so I called: "Sid, are you alright?" The answer came loud and clear: "Of course I'm alright, but I have my shirt stuck in my zip and I can't get the damn thing up or down." I shouted back: "I can't come in there. You will have to come outside. It is quite dark, so no one will see you." Then began the struggle to release the shirt from the zip, first one pulling and tugging, then the other having a go. All the time Sid was fuming, saying: "I'll never buy another pair of trousers with a zip while ever I live," and "Don't you ever buy me a pair either." After a few more pulls the shirt was released with a terrible rending sound, and Sid tucked away the torn remnants of his shirt flap back into his trousers, and we hastened back into the hall.

2

Marriages and Deaths

IT was with great delight that we heard the news that Sid's sister Kathleen had become engaged to Vincent Sibley, head of the physical education department at Loughborough College. Vin had lost his wife around the same time that Kath's husband had been killed. He had twin children, a boy and a girl. After they were married Kath became a wonderful mother to these children, who in turn loved her almost as though she was really their own mother. Both our own family and people in the village missed Kathleen very much, but she was living only five miles away in Loughborough, so we met quite often. My children loved to spend a holiday with them, and the twins, Diana and Michael, would stay with us at the farm while Kath and Vin had a holiday on their own. Kath would come over most weeks to visit her parents, and she and her mother would very often spend a few hours with us at the farm. These visits were much enjoyed, we had such lovely natters together, and I still look back on them as a very happy time in our lives. After several years Kath had a baby boy of her own, whom she named Robert. Diana, her stepdaughter, emigrated to America as a nurse, and later her stepson Michael entered college to study engineering.

One morning my father-in-law was cycling home from our farm when a dog ran out of a gateway, bringing him heavily off his cycle. He was unconscious and was taken into the house opposite where his sister Nan lived. The doctor was sent for, and he ordered him three complete days in bed. This father would not do. The doctor tried persuasion, but father said he was alright and he had far too much work to do to stay in bed. The doctor said: "I can't make you, Mr Smith, but I think you will regret not doing so, as anybody your age, after suffering the slightest concussion, should have complete rest for three days." Whether things would have been different, had he obeyed the doctor, one cannot tell, but from the day of that cycle accident father gradually deteriorated.

About this time I became pregnant with my fourth child — a subject to which I shall return in my next chapter. Two months before my baby was due, father-in-law collapsed in the bathroom. He fell backwards into the bath while shaving. In spite of good nursing, he never recovered, and we lost our beloved father. He had been a man who had given his life working hard in the service of our village and its people. For example, he spent hours in the evenings filling in forms for people. The following was written in our local paper which tells how much he was missed by so many:

Loughborough Loses a Fine Odd Fellow
A Well Known Public Figure

Odd Fellows in the Loughborough District regret the death of Brother John Smith, P.P.G.M., which took place at "Edgcumbe," Wymeswold, on Thursday, August 1st, after a prolonged illness. He was in his 72nd year. He was well known in Leicester agricultural circles, and retired from the family holding in 1934.

Up to his death Mr. Smith was a member of the Barrow-on-Soar Rural District Council. He was also a member of the old Loughborough Rural District Council for many years, occupying the chair in 1934. Until last year he was for over 35 years secretary of the Sun Lodge (Wymeswold) and had attained the highest honour which the District could give him, that of Provincial Grand Master. He was also a District arbitrator and served on the District Management Committee for many years. His work for the Odd Fellows had been marked by the recommendation that he should be awarded the jewel for meritorious service.

He was chairman of the Parish Council, a school manager and a trustee of the Wymeswold Consolidated Charities and of the Memorial Hall. In 1937 he was appointed a Justice of the Peace.

Until last Easter he was people's

warden of St. Mary's Parish Church. A keen bowler, he was a member of the Wymeswold Bowling Club. He leaves a widow, two sons, and a daughter.

The funeral took place at Wymeswold on Sunday, August 4, the Vicar, the Rev. P. R. Harvey, officiating, in the presence of a large number of representatives of public bodies and other sympathisers.

AN APPRECIATION

The passing of John Smith has brought the realisation, not only to his native village but to the whole community, of which he took such a large share, how very ill he could be spared at this peculiar time in our history, and how very difficult it will be to fill his place. Those who worked with him in the Friendly Society Movement know that his whole outlook in life was to try to do some good to others. The position he reached amplified the trust and confidence in which he was held by all who knew him. In the village, whatever the problem, everyone said: "Go to John Smith, he will help and put you right if he can." And so through numerous ways he always strove to obey the Divine Command of Him he worshipped. — "Do unto others as ye would they should do to you." Steadfast and loyal to the Church, to his Odd Fellows' Lodge and District, and to any movement to which he belonged, he endeavoured always to stand up for his principles. During the war his thoughts and actions were always for others, and his devotion to the work of the Royal Observation Corps during those trying years, is known to many as a service of devotion and unselfishness. As Chairman of the Parish Council he was always courteous and scrupulously fair. As a magistrate all his actions and decisions were arrived at by a most careful consideration of the facts. As the large and representative congregation of so many sections of the community stood in that old village church and heard those comforting words: "I am the Resurrection and the Life," we felt how truly John had

lived in his Faith, and the good he had done in playing his part would never be lost. The procession through the village, now strangely hushed, saw the tribute of those who had lived and worked with him, so manifest; every blind drawn in respect, and so as the last solemn rites were ended we salute the memory of one who, as everyone who knew him said: "He was a good man." What greater tribute is needed.
W. A. KEY, P.P.G.M.

I was unable to attend the funeral service because of my condition, but Sid told me afterwards that our village church was filled with people from far and near, who had come to pay their respects to such a good man.

A year or two after my fourth pregnancy, Sid decided I should have a week's holiday, so we left his brother Bob and our eldest son Sidney in charge of the farm, and went to Skegness, a seaside town on the east coast. Tragically our holiday was terminated the day after we arrived. We were upstairs at our hotel when the daughter of the house came up to say Sid was wanted urgently on the phone. She did not say who wanted him, but we could see she was greatly upset. I sat for what seemed an age, thinking of all sorts of things that might have happened at home. The worst thought was whether Sidney had had an accident with a new gun we had recently bought him. I knew by Sid's face the news was bad. He came straight out with it. He said: "Mother has just died in her sleep." It was my brother Warner who rang, and he said Kath and Bob, Sid's brother and sister, were so upset they needed us at home. We quietly and quickly repacked all our belongings, and started for home. I shall never forget that awful journey. We travelled through one of the worst thunderstorms which lasted nearly all the way home. Sometimes we had to stop the car: the rain was so bad we could not see our way.

We arrived home to find Kathleen and Bob in a shocked, dazed condition. We learned that Grandma Smith had cooked her usual Sunday dinner, along with a batch of pastry and a sandwich cake, after which she had washed everything up. Then she had said to Bob: "We will go to bed for an hour or so, and I will wake you up when it is time to go to the farm for milking." Bob woke up, and thought it was funny his mother had not yet woken him as promised. He went into his mother's bedroom and found she had died peacefully in her sleep during the afternoon.

We all missed our Grandma Smith. Kath was a long time before she got over the shock. Bob, who was living at his mother's after divorcing his wife, was about to remarry. He inherited his mother's house along with a field, where he started a small poultry farm as a supplement to his wages for working on our farm. Eventually he built up a business producing eggs and selling them on an egg-round in Loughborough. From his first marriage Bob had a girl named Barbara. His second marriage produced two sons: a right young Turk named John and another boy they called Norman. These three were always great friends with my younger children. The boys spent a number of their summer holidays on our farm, in preference to a holiday at the seaside with their parents. During my lifetime I have noticed continually that a large majority of children prefer a holiday on a farm, where there are so many animals, to a holiday at the seaside. Rarely did a summer holiday go by without a number of our relatives staying at our place. I have always loved children, and welcomed them to stay with their country cousins. I had one nephew who spent every Christmas, Easter and summer holiday with us. A few days before the end of each holiday he would go extremely quiet until he managed to blurt out: "Auntie Nell, can I come here for the next school holiday?" After a favourable answer of "Of course you can, Norman", he became his old happy self again.

After the sad loss of our Grandma Smith life on the farm settled down to a busy routine, with Bob only part time, but with our elder son Sidney doing more and more jobs. Sidney was always a splendid and dedicated worker. From an early age all he ever wanted was to be out on the farm. One day he was at the Wymeswold Flower Show and Gymkhana where he spent most of the time with a beautiful girl from Chester named Mary Brennand. Actually Mary's mother was my second cousin, who had been brought up in Wymeswold, but met and married a boy living in Chester. They had two girls: Mary and Helen. Every summer holiday these two spent most of their time in Wymeswold with their mother's sister who had a smallholding in Wymeswold, which was very near to our farm. The two families were all friends, meeting quite often as country people do. The friendship between Sidney and Mary deepened over the years, and they started going steady. Mary had done her teacher's training at Goldsmiths' College, London, then obtained a teaching job, first at Kirkby-in-Ashfield, then at Shepshed, a large village a few miles the other side of Loughborough.

Mary had been teaching for four years when a farmer named Mills retired from a hundred and fifty acre farm owned by Trinity College, Cambridge. This was a very desirable farm which Sidney said he would like to take over. We all thought this wonderful chance had come a couple of years too soon. Sidney was only twenty-two years old, and he and Mary had not contemplated marriage just at that time. Sidney decided to apply to Trinity for tenancy of the farm. A letter of application was written, and he was put on a long list of applicants along with one of his best friends named Harry Mills. Then, because of the uncertainty of Sidney and Mary getting married, another letter was written to Trinity withdrawing his application for the farm. I had this letter in my pocket and was on my way to the post office, but decided first to call on our Aunt Nan who was unwell. I stayed for a while talking to Aunt Nan, when Sidney knocked on the window to ask if I had posted the letter. I said: "No, not yet." Sidney breathed a great sigh of relief. He said: "Please don't, not yet. Mary and I are going up to Chester to have a talk with her parents about the farm."

What a difference not posting this letter made to Sidney and Mary's life! They returned home from Chester with the news that they would be getting married in around six months time, and they hoped very much they would be the next tenants of Clay House Farm. In due course we heard that Sidney and his friend Harry Mills were the two short-listed ones for the farm. Trinity College's agents said they could not possibly decide between these two. Both were suitable tenants, both their families had farmed a Trinity farm for three generations, and were good farmers who paid their rents when due. So they decided to come over to the vacant farm and meet the two young men. They were going to put their names in a hat, spin a coin, and one of them would pick a name out. That name would be the next tenant of the farm. How a slip of paper changed their lives! The two young men, along with their fathers, met the agent down at the Clay House Farm. Sidney was so excited he could hardly speak. He said the suspense was awful, waiting for the draw to take place. At last the names were placed in the hat and the coin was spun to see who should draw. Harry was the one and he drew out Sidney's name. Harry, like a good friend, turned to Sidney, shook his hand, and wished him all the luck in the world, and hoped he would prosper on the farm. Everything turned out well for both these boys.

During the next few years Sidney and Mary worked so hard on the farmhouse which was very large, having four main rooms downstairs with two kitchens, five bedrooms, a bathroom, and a small washroom. Sidney and one man named Ernest Bates, who had worked on the farm for years, managed one hundred acres of the original farm, the other fifty acres being transferred to our farm, making it about 140 acres. Sidney spent all his working hours at Clay House Farm, but ate and slept at home until he married.

Sidney and Mary were married in Mary's home town of Chester. The colours of Mary's dress and veil were the palest of pale pink and the dress material was embossed satin. Mary is very tall, with black wavy hair. Never did I see a more elegant bride. The bridesmaids — Helen, Mary's sister, who was chief bridesmaid, our Lizbeth, and Heather, a small cousin of Mary's — all were dressed in pale blue. This wedding was a happy occasion for everyone, it was so obvious that theirs would be a good marriage. After the service at St. Oswald's Church, and a reception held at the Blossoms Hotel, we saw the happy couple off for their honeymoon at Minehead, and then the cars started for home.

On nearing the end of our journey my brother Warner took a wrong turning. Sid followed but we realized the mistake first and stopped. Warner found his mistake immediately afterwards, turned into a gateway, and backed out to turn around, but unfortunately backed straight into an oncoming car. Now Warner always believed the best method of defence was attack. He jumped out and asked the other driver what the devil he thought he was doing. He took this calmly, and asked Warner for his name and address. Afterwards they settled it out of court, Warner paying up. Our son David, who was in the car, remembers Sybil saying to her husband a few miles after they left the scene of the accident: "You know, you were in the wrong, Warner."

3

The Twins

WHEN Sid and I were well into our thirties, we decided we would like to have another baby in the hope that this time we would at last get a girl. I was only seven weeks pregnant when I first thought I was carrying twins. On a visit to my parents I asked mother if we had ever had twins in our family. She said she only knew of one set of twins several generations back and asked: "But Nell, why do you ask?" I said: "Look at me, mother, and I am only seven weeks pregnant." "Goodness me!" says mum, "you really do look like it." When I was nine weeks pregnant, I asked the district nurse to call and see me when she was in the village. Our district nurse served several villages on the wolds, including Burton, Prestwold, Hoton, Cotes and Wymeswold. The nurse lived in a cottage at Hoton owned by Sir Edward Packe, whose estate covered most of the land around these villages. She came one evening to see me. "What is the matter, Mrs Smith?" she asked. I answered: "I am not ill, nurse, but will you examine me to see if I'm carrying twins?" As she performed this examination, she asked how far gone I was. When I told her only nine weeks, she could not believe me, but at each monthly examination she still maintained there were no twins and that I must be wrong in my reckoning.

In due course we had to think about buying a pram, as I had given the old one away. For months we tried to buy one. Our names were on several waiting lists, but buying a pram in those first post-war years was almost impossible, so few were being made. I began to think we would not get one in time, when one night I had a dream that I went into a shop, and there before my eyes was a lovely coach-built cream pram with a brown hood and apron. While having breakfast I told my dream to the family. Sid said: "Perhaps you'd better nip down to Loughborough and try once again to buy a pram. Your dream might be a good omen." We were not really believers in either good or bad omens, but I got out the car, and hopefully set out for Loughborough. I first went to the shop where we had bought our first pram, and where we were known. The assistant said: "Sorry, no. We have not had one in for weeks, but our van has just gone to the station, and there might be a very slight chance of one being there with the rest of our orders." He said: "Call back in about one hour." Their long waiting list for prams had been scrapped, and each one that came in was sold to the first customer to arrive. They found that the list had been too difficult to keep: some people had left the town, some had bought second-hand prams. They found that the time and expense involved in tracing these customers were more than they could manage. Having had that dream, I thought I would stay in the shop until their furniture van came back from the station. As the van drew up, I went out of the shop to meet it, but with very little hope of finding a pram among the furniture. I watched the men open the huge back doors of the van, and there, to my delighted surprise, was a beautiful maroon-coloured pram. I raced inside to Mr Hughes almost shouting: "They have one. May I have it?" "Of course you may," he said. "You are definitely the first customer." I paid for the pram and it was loaded on to the back of my car, which in those days had a let-down boot. My family was so pleased to see me arrive home with the longed-for pram.

Three weeks before my baby was due, both our young doctor and our district nurse came to give me a final examination. The doctor suddenly said: "It is twins, nurse." The nurse answered: "No, I don't think it is. I have only heard one heartbeat on each examination I have made." Then they went into a conversation full of medical terms which I could not understand. Still they disagreed. Finally the doctor said: "Nurse, if Mrs Smith doesn't have twins, I will attend this confinement free of charge." (We paid our doctor in those days.) He said he could not hear two heartbeats but he was sure that just once he had felt two heads. Now, after telling them from nine weeks of pregnancy that I thought it was twins, I felt a bit put out. I thought of my lovely new pram that would not be big enough, and wondered where in the wide world I would obtain a twin pram. The doctor said: "One way to make sure would be an X-ray." So off to Loughborough Hospital Sid took me. He waited outside until I had the result. I will never forget my excitement when they showed me the X-ray plate. There they lay, the bigger twin curled around the smaller twin. As I walked out down the hospital steps I cried excitedly to Sid who was across the other side of the road: "It's twins, Sid; it really is." Then I realized that people passing by had stopped in their tracks, and were smiling at the sight of this huge woman being hugged by her husband, because they had just learned they were having twins.

After the excitement had died down a bit and we had sat in our car until at least I became normal again, we went to the shop where I had bought the pram and asked Mr Hughes if he would take it back. He was quite flabbergasted to think

I did not want the pram, but he said he would take it back, and that it would be resold immediately. When I told him I was having twins, and asked where I could buy a twin pram, he smiled and said: "That is quite alright. A twin pram has priority. We will order one and it will be six weeks delivery." This was a great relief to me. We then had to do quite a bit more shopping, as two babies needed double the clothes and nappies. I arrived home that day exhausted by excitement and shopping, but had revived sufficiently the following day to start knitting extra garments, so my babies would both be dressed in the same kind of clothes.

As I was having my babies at home, my sister Lottie and I spring-cleaned our bedroom, putting all clean clothes on our bed and washing the furniture. That evening I was washing up the supper pots around 10:15 when I felt things had started. I called Bill and Phyll who were living with us at that time, and while Sid got the doctor and nurse, they helped me get ready for bed. After a bath I was snug and warm, but with pains that were too frequent for my liking. How I wished the doctor and nurse were with me! But I had not long to wait. First the nurse arrived and did everything in readiness for the doctor who was not long coming.

Just after midnight I gave birth . . . yes, to another boy, weighing six and half pounds! The nurse called downstairs to tell them the first was a boy. I was chattering away, jokingly saying: "The next has just got to be a girl." Eleven and a half minutes later a five-pound baby girl was born. This baby had had what they called a "shock birth", which meant she had been born too quickly, receiving a slight concussion. She was also in the last stages of asphyxia, drowned by fluid from the first birth. I went very quiet praying hard that my baby girl would be revived. The doctor immediately started artificial respiration. On such a small body this was done with the first finger and thumb of each hand. The baby was given two injections for the heart, and when the doctors' fingers became numb, the nurse took over. When the doctor started again, the nurse came to me to see if I was alright. I whispered: "Yes,

I'm quite alright," although I knew I was not. The next time she looked at me she saw what I was trying to hide: I was suffering a massive haemorrhage. I begged her to leave me and help with the baby who had just made a slight sound. She said she had not heard the sound, but I knew I had. She hesitated, realizing she had been taught to save the mother first. I pleaded with her, saying I could buy more bedclothes, all of which were saturated up to my neck, but I could not buy another baby girl. At that moment the doctor said: "The baby is alive, but I don't know if she will recover."

By this time the family waiting downstairs was in a dreadful state. Everything had gone dead quiet, after my joking about the next must be a girl. Sid could not stand the strain any longer. He called upstairs: "Is everything alright?" The nurse answered: "Your wife has had a little girl, Mr Smith, but we don't know yet if she is going to be alright. She has not come round yet." Afterwards Sid told me that hour was the worst of his life, as he had mistakenly thought it was I who had not come round.

The doctor was wonderful. He raced down to Loughborough Hospital for a cylinder of oxygen. The baby girl was put in cotton wool under a kind of see-through tent with the oxygen fixed. Every few hours for three days the nurse sucked through a catheter the mucus from the baby's lungs. The doctor stayed with the baby girl while the nurse looked after me. Then the poor little baby boy, who had been left in his cot with only a warmed flannel around him, was picked up by the nurse who bathed and dressed him. She stayed all night watching over my baby girl who was moaning so quietly with every laboured breath. The nurse kept saying: "If only she would cry, I know she would be alright." During the next day the nurse was called away to another birth, but as soon as it was over, back she came. Her first question was: "Has the baby cried yet?" She was so disappointed when told she had not. The nurse did her rounds, but spent the rest of her time with me, until the baby cried. The doctor said she would manage now without the oxygen, and the nurse then bathed her in olive oil, again clothing her in cotton wool. I breast-fed both my babies, but at first I was too weak to sit up, and Sid, bless him, sat on the bed and held me up while I fed them. The nurse helped me in the daytime, Sid at night. After the fifth day our baby girl was crying lustily, and both the doctor and nurse thought she would completely recover. We named her Elizabeth Helen, but she was always called Lizbeth. Her twin brother, an example of a perfect baby, we called Richard Gordon.

Lizbeth was now restored to normality, both babies were feeding well, the girl every three hours, the boy every four hours, and I was getting stronger day by day. We had reason to think our troubles were over, but no, we had a very serious six weeks before us because of problems with our boy twin. I was kept in bed for two weeks to recover. Our regular nurse went on vacation for ten days after the birth, necessitating a relief nurse to attend the twins for three days. It was after the relief nurse had been twice to bath the twins that, on changing baby Richard's nappy at the 6 a.m. feed, I noticed two small blisters, the size of a match-head. I immediately thought the nurse had accidentally spilt a couple of spots of hot water on his thigh. (She was furious with me for thinking this.) When the nurse stripped him for his bath, Richard had five blisters on his thigh. I could see that the nurse was greatly alarmed. She re-nappied him without bathing him, and urgently called Sid to ring the doctor immediately. There was no answer so he took a note to the surgery in the village asking for an immediate visit to see Richard. The doctor never came that day, but the nurse called through the window to hear what the doctor had said. She seemed petrified when told he had not been. She told Sid to go to Costock, a village three miles away where our doctor was resident and not to come home without him, as she thought this was a very serious case, and that she could not even enter the house because of the infection. By now I was deeply worried about baby Richard, as he now had a multitude of blisters all over his thighs.

When Sid arrived at the house, the doctor was on the point of leaving for a new practice in the north of England, but when Sid told him of the nurse's fear for the baby, he immediately came and examined him. He too was deeply worried, as he said he had only seen this kind of thing once in his career. Previously there had been no cure, but penicillin might kill the bacteria. That kind young man disinfected himself and then went to buy some penicillin ointment, which he left at the house with instructions on how to use it. During the next twenty-four hours my lovely baby had blisters all over his buttocks, and a few had appeared on his tummy. The new doctor, a much older man, came to see him the next day, and although he did not touch the baby, he completely disinfected himself before leaving the house, but he had told me just what to do for the best. At every nappy change I had to hold a sterilized needle in one hand, and prick every blister I could find, one by one, and with a piece of cotton wool in the other hand wipe off the poisoned fluid and burn it instantly. The great fear was that baby Lizbeth would catch this killing disease called pemphigus. I took great trouble to avoid this. I used to feed the baby girl first — she was now on four-hourly feeding, thank God — bath and dress her, then put her away in a cot as far from baby Richard as possible. Then Richard, who was dressed in just a vest and nappy, with a huge sheet doubled up around him, was fed. Then this awful job of pricking every new blister and burning the fluid instantly began all over again. Sometimes there were literally dozens of tiny blisters, so minute they were on a piece of skin the size of a new penny. Then after spreading the penicillin ointment all over him, I nappied him and I wrapped him in a clean sheet again. Everything was then put into disinfectant and I myself bathed and put on clean clothes. This had to be done every four hours during the day, and once during the night.

I was indeed lucky to have many kind friends. My sister Lottie looked after my family, and a lady named Mrs Tyler came every day and did all the washing. Mrs Tyler went six weeks without coming into contact with her own grandchildren to enable her to give me such valuable help. For ten days we did not know if

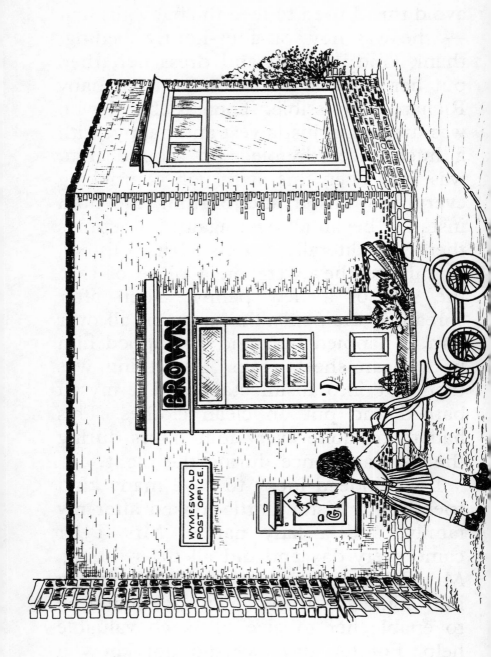

we would win this battle of the blisters, but after that time one could perceive a gradual improvement. After four weeks there was only the odd new blister. Our prayers were answered as regards baby Lizbeth who never caught the disease.

When our own nurse was allowed to come into our house, she sat down and talked a long time about pemphigus. She had only seen it once, and had been horrified when told Richard had it, and yet she was not allowed to come near him. The nurse said that when she was learning her midwifery, a baby in the ward was diagnosed as having pemphigus. After twenty-four hours all the babies had caught it, and regrettably they all died. The ward was isolated, and no more confinements were admitted. Without that miracle drug penicillin my baby Richard would have died too, and I would never have known the great joy of raising my beautiful twin babies.

By the time we were cleared of the contamination the twin-pram had arrived in Loughborough. Although I was very tired after our eight-week ordeal, I was so proud to take our first walk out with the twins, with young Michael running alongside. For six months all my time was taken up with looking after the twins and cooking for my family. Lottie did the cleaning and my friend Mrs Tyler did the washing. My twins were the first to be born in the village for over twenty-seven years. This meant that, when I took them out, nearly everyone we met stopped to look at them. This got so bad that I had to stop taking them regularly down to the village. Instead I took them up the lane where we could be quieter, but there it meant an awfully steep hill to climb before reaching the level ground again.

Once when we were on holiday with Michael and the twins, we found Lizbeth had disappeared while we were walking on the pathway in the main shopping street. Sid went one way, while I hastened the other way. She was found pushing a doll's pram, which she had taken from outside a huge toy-shop. We rushed back to the shop, feeling we might be accused of stealing the pram. When we explained to the owner that our three-year-old Lizbeth had walked off with the pram, he smiled, saying: "It's not the first time a child has done that." Sid said: "Well, Lizbeth seems to think it belongs to her, we'd better buy it for her." When she was a little older, we bought a much bigger doll's pram, but she seldom used it for her dolls. She used to dress up her kittens in doll's clothes and tuck them into the pram. They loved riding in it. I think Lizbeth must have walked miles with those kittens, if all her walks were added up.

The twins loved playing outside. When it rained, we had to place a board into grooves at the back door to keep them in. When we were young, we must have been fresh-air worshippers, because we lived with the kitchen door wide open except in severe winter weather, and our bedroom window was never shut, only in foggy weather. My babies always slept outside in their prams.

4

Children and Animals

AS our twins grew older, they became an increasing joy to all the family. They were a delight to watch when they played with each other. I shall always remember a conversation between them as they sat in the bath together, which I overheard as I was nearing the bathroom. Richard was saying "Leeby (he always called Lizbeth Leeby), I hate to hurt people's feelings. It gives me a pain just here" (pointing to his chest). "Do you know," answered Lizbeth, "it gives me a pain there, too, when I hurt anyone's feelings." They shared everything they had given to them. Once Richard was playing on the lawn in the front of the house when the lady across the road gave him a sweet. "Oh Farney," he said, "haven't you got one for Leeby too?" Mrs. Farnsworth said: "Lizbeth isn't here so I didn't bring her one." Richard told her that if he had a sweet, she must bring Leeby one or he could not have one.

I dressed the twins alike until they went to school. Then Richard showed strong signs that he did not want to be dressed in the same colours as Lizbeth. I used to make all their clothes. Lizbeth's skirts were the same colour and material as Richard's trousers, with shirt blouses exactly the same, but this had to be stopped when Richard, small as he was, objected so strongly.

Children brought up on farms are lucky indeed: they enjoy many kinds of pets. Our children had dogs, cats and rabbits, and once Michael brought up a jackdaw by hand. This bird kept to Michael only. He would go to school with him, sitting on his shoulder, and when Michael went into school, Jacky would fly home again, but he would always be ready to meet Michael again out of school. Jacky became great friends with our sheepdog, Rover, and with two kittens belonging to Richard and Lizbeth. Often they would be found asleep together on the lawn, Jacky cuddling up between them, sometimes sitting on Rover's head. Our one fear was that a strange cat would kill Jacky, because he trusted our cats. Eventually this was what happened. He had one narrow escape with a huge black cat. From my bedroom window I heard Jacky squawking. On looking outside, I saw this black cat waiting to spring at Jacky, who was sitting on a low pigsty door. I screamed at the cat which ran away, but eventually Jacky was killed, no doubt by this cat. A lot of feathers was all that was left.

We knew this cat was a killer. We had found it killing many of our chicks, but it always evaded our attempts to catch it. After it had killed around eighty chicks, we discovered its owner by following it home. The owner refused to destroy his cat, so we asked the police to advise him about this matter. He was told he would have to pay for the eighty month-old chicks it had killed, and any other future chicks it killed. After learning this, he had the cat put down.

We had another big loss of chicks caused by a huge black and white stray tom-cat. Neighbours all around us were losing chicks, but no one had a gun handy when the cat was at its dirty work. However, one day an old lady came panting up the yard, saying she had got the killer cat penned in her yard behind a huge water-butt. Sid's brother Bob picked up a gun and quickly made his way after the old lady. She showed him where the cat was, and quickly escaped into her house, not wanting to see a cat killed at close range. Bob could just see the cat, but had only a small space to fix the gun. Fortunately, he killed it instantly with a shot through the head.

After these huge losses of chicks to marauding cats, we used large cages made with wood and wire. We used these until the chicks were older and stood a better chance of escaping this dreadful end.

In the old days defenceless young chicks, reared outside, faced dreadful and horrific dangers, even when stationed near the farmyard. At one time a magpie with her own chicks in a nest up a pear-tree in our orchard fetched and killed a couple of chicks every day until, in real desperation, Sid asked a neighbour's boy, who was good at climbing trees, to come to his aid by climbing this huge pear-tree and removing these fully-fledged baby magpies. The mother abandoned the nest and we never saw her again. The boy received 2/6 for his good work, which in those days was a full-grown man's two hours' pay. He was, of course, absolutely delighted with such a large sum, racing home to tell his mum. But we did not know of his mum's displeasure until years afterwards, when she told me her young son had torn his good school coat while climbing the tree, and she had had that to mend.

If only the animal rights campaigners realized that the new ways of rearing and keeping poultry are far better than the old haphazard ways of the past, and actually the birds suffer less hazards and sheer cruelty of circumstances beyond the control of poultry farmers. Being an old lady of seventy-five years with tremendous experience of both ways, I know without any doubt that controlled environment is better both for man and birds. If the country reverted back to everything on free range, the next generation of do-gooders would be campaigning for the return of controlled environment!

When I was a child, and even up to the time of my marriage, chicks were raised by setting around fourteen fertilized eggs under a hen that had become broody. She would then patiently sit on them for three weeks, turning each egg over in turn, only getting off the nest once a day to eat and drink. During the last few days the nesting hens refused to leave their eggs. If they were lifted off the nest and put down against their water and meal, they would quickly snatch a little of each and back they would go to their eggs. Nature is a very wonderful thing. When the chicks were all hatched, and had become dry and fluffy, both hen and chicks were taken outside and placed into coops the size of a small dog kennel, but with slatted fronts to enable the chicks to run around on the earth. Food and water were readily available at all times where the mother hen could put out her head to reach them. If the weather became wet or cold, the chicks would shelter under their mother, as they did every night until they grew too big. Then the mother would turn against her chicks and they would have to be taken away from her. When incubators came on the market, and foster mothers called hoovers, nature's way was discontinued, and when a hen became broody, she was shut up on a wire floor where she soon got over her broodiness.

Only once in all our years of farming did we see the dreadful sight of a young healthy cow with the whole of her womb in the gutter, and we had never heard of this happening anywhere else. It happened like this.

The cow was a well-bred Friesian which had delivered her calf quite normally without any complications whatsoever. We were delighted with both mother and calf until Sid went into the cowshed later on and saw this awful bloody mess lying there. He came into the house white-faced and really upset, saying: "Nell, I have never seen anything like this in all my life. Will you ring for the vet?" I rang immediately, but Mr Bryson, who usually came to our farm, was out on another case, so a young man just out of college, who had obtained a job as an assistant to Mr Bryson, came instead. Oh dear! That poor young man with Sid's help tried for one and a half hours to replace that repulsive mass back inside the cow, but failed miserably. He gave up and dejectedly washed up and went back to the surgery to report his failure to replace the womb.

Sid and I were so troubled. Whatever could we do? We did not want to lose such a valuable animal, but we thought there was nothing else for it but to have her put down. We stood in stricken silence at what this poor young cow must be enduring, when suddenly we heard a car draw into the yard and, with a screeching of brakes, Mr Bryson leaped out, calling for hot water and a clean sterile sheet. By the time I got them there, Mr Bryson was already dressed in his oilskin overalls. First they spread my lovely clean sheet along the gutter. Then they eased that whole dreadful mess onto it. Then in a most professional manner Mr Bryson eased the whole womb back into the cow. We all breathed a great sigh of relief, but that poor cow's ordeal

was not yet over, for the whole opening was then stitched up, to stop the womb falling out once again. I was handed my mucky bloody sheet to wash, but I just could not face that job, so we burned the whole mess. When the vet placed it under the cow, I thought: "Ah! Some sterilized sheet after the whole lot has lain in the gutter for several hours!" I always remember Mr Bryson's words as he washed down: "That job needed a real man." It sure did, but that poor cow died after all that suffering.

Michael and the twins had many friends who came in the evenings and at holiday times to play in the farmyard and outbuildings. I encouraged these friends, as I thought it was much safer for them to play there than on the streets. One thing I was very strict about: no swearing was allowed and the punishment was to be sent home. Usually they were all reasonably good, but one day I could hear a quarrel starting, so I kept an eye and an ear on them. Suddenly one little chappie let out an awful mouthful of swear words, so I asked who was that saying such bad words. No one let on the name but I knew who it was, so I called to him: "Out, laddie." I can see that child now in my mind's eye, sliving out the yard, and into the street. Then he popped his head round the gatepost and shouted: "The wust of you is, Missus, ya swank so." I was tickled pink at the thought that this little lad thought it was swanking because I would not allow swearing in our yard.

A farmyard is a children's paradise with so many things around, numerous hiding places, and stacks to climb, not to mention all the pets they have at different times. Riding on top of a load of hay was another favourite pastime. Those we called the regulars were often quite helpful in many ways. One of the jobs they loved doing was catching pullets ready for moving into their laying quarters. As one child said: "Yes, and we love the money you pay us, Missus."

Early one morning an amusing incident occurred involving our Richard. His father watched him sleepily walking up the yard to feed a few hens he kept for himself. Sid said: "Where are you going, Richard?" "I'm going to feed my hens," answered Richard. "Oh," said his father, "What are you feeding them with?" Richard looked down into his bucket. All he had in it was hot water. Poor lad, he was so sleepy he had not mixed the meal into the water.

Richard was just like our son David used to be: an absentminded professor. I once took David to buy a pair of flannel trousers, where a short, fat man was also buying a pair. David at that time was six feet tall. To cut a long story short, David picked up the short man's parcel. The next day he put on the new trousers, and was going to leave for Loughborough, when a friend said to him: "Hey up, David! Whose trousers have you got on?" "Oh!" answered David, "they are a new pair my mum bought me." After looking down to find a pair of trousers that only just covered the knee and would have held another David in the waist, he hurriedly ran upstairs to change into his old ones.

Another funny thing happened to Richard when he lay on his back, playing with a threepenny piece, throwing it up in the air as high as possible and trying to

catch it again. He did this once too often: the coin fell into his open mouth and he swallowed it. This really frightened him. First it was fast in his throat, then he kept pointing to his chest, saying: "It's here now," then: "It's lower down now," until suddenly he cried: "It's gone now." I rang the doctor who said I must watch for the coin in his motions. I told Richard he must run home from school if the need arose. For three or four days I examined the motions minutely, but no coin emerged. The doctor decided he must have an X-ray. This meant a journey to Nottingham Hospital. The result of the X-ray: no coin! This puzzled us for many weeks, until Richard confessed he had once been taken short at school and forgotten to run home.

Lizbeth was pony mad. She was always asking: "May I have a pony, daddy?" So when Sid bought a lovely pony at the Loughborough fair, bringing it home in the trailer behind the car, he stopped at the school and asked if Lizbeth could be let out for a few minutes. When she saw this tiny pony, her excitement knew no bounds. She named it Merrylegs, and then it was sent to Jane Glass's riding school to be broken in for riding. This pony was so small Sid could pick it up off all four feet, but as Lizbeth grew so did the pony, and she enjoyed many happy years riding it.

Some years later, we invested in a few in-lamb ewes. Sid decided to buy around twenty cross-bred old ewes, and I bought ten pure-bred young ones. We had never had any experience keeping sheep. We wrongly thought they did not need much attention: they would graze and manure the ground. A good farmer knew his grass land benefited by a change of animals grazing it. Very little artificial fertilizer was used in our early days of farming. We found that sheep, in fact, needed quite a lot of attention. For example, they suffered from foot rot which was a very smelly disease. Flies also caused a lot of trouble. Sometimes during hot weather they would "strike the sheep", laying their eggs on the hind part of the animal. In a very short time the eggs would hatch, and the sheep would be made exceedingly uncomfortable by maggots eating their way into the flesh. Nowadays one is obliged by law to have them dipped. We used to take our sheep to a farmer friend who owned a sheep dip, but in my younger days a man named Mr Blount used to dam up the brook at the bottom of London Lane. In a kind of pond which formed, Mr Blount used to stand in a huge barrel, taking each sheep in turn from the farmer who owned it, and literally dipping the animal several times right under the treated water. The farmers had to arrange to come in their turns to avoid congestion of sheep around this homemade sheep-dip.

Sid's twenty-year-old ewes did splendidly. Most of them had two lambs each, and some had three. We took away one lamb from all those that had three and the children brought them up on a bottle. But they became so cade they followed us everywhere we went, which was a great nuisance. They even followed the children to school, and we had to fetch them back home. When they were let out into the field, they escaped, wandering all over the village. Friends were always ringing us up, saying: "Your lambs are with us. Can you fetch them?" Sometimes they were lost for days, but they always came back, or were brought back by neighbours, often from many miles away.

My ten young pure-bred sheep were a disaster. I finished up with only five lambs, with ten mothers. Many lambs were stillborn, others were so weak they never managed to suckle. Needless to say I did not give these mothers a second chance. They were fattened and sold. This was the first and last time I bought sheep. But Sid's old ewes did well for several more years, until they had to be sold because their teeth fell out, and they could not eat properly. One year we had seven extra lambs, which their mothers could not feed. The children were delighted to rear them. When they were seven weeks old, we put them in a friend's orchard for three hours, where we think they ate something which poisoned them. Five of them died and two survived. The children were dreadfully upset at these deaths. Each lamb was buried in the garden, with small stones over them, with a wooden cross at each one and their names printed on it.

5

The Coming of Television

WHEN the twins were three years old, television came to our part of the country. London had had it for some time. Jim Taylor and Sid each decided to have a television. They were the only sets in the village for a long time. I well remember that when the F.A. Cup final was televised, our living-kitchen was crammed full. The tallest stood in rows at the back, then the next tallest, and so on until the youngest were sitting on the floor just in front of the television. There were over forty people watching that match in a room eighteen feet by sixteen feet. It was a wet day and when they all left, my living-room floor was a muddy mess, but oh! how they had enjoyed seeing that match actually taking place. Lads I hardly knew came to ask if they could come and watch. Nearly all wanted to know how much they owed me.

When I said: "Nothing, you're welcome," they were quite embarrassed.

Another happy television story, very different from a football match with boys and men watching, was about two old ladies living near our farm who were right good royalists. One was an old spinster named Sally Collington. The other was eighty-year-old Ma Blount, the sheep-dipper's widow, always lovingly called Ma, never Mrs, who in her earlier day had sold sweets from her tiny cottage. These two lived next door to each other in two very old cottages, one room up and one room down. They had never had water or electricity installed in their cottages, and both lived the life of fifty years ago. The time came when our late King and his Queen, now the Queen Mother, were to be on television, meeting the French president and his wife at a London station. I thought how nice it would be for these two dedicated royalists to see the King and Queen on television, so I invited them to a homemade pork-pie tea, and to see their King and Queen. They were delighted and, dressed in their Sunday-best clothes, arrived promptly at the time stated. They sat in our warm comfortable living-kitchen, speechless and enthralled. I got more pleasure watching their dear old faces than watching the television.

When it was all over, I asked them to sit down at the table and said I would put the kettle on for a cuppa, and do some toast to eat with the pork pie. I turned on my electric kettle which was sitting in the hearth a few inches from the fire. Ma Blount was longing for a cup of tea after all the excitement, and was getting quite worried about the kettle. At last she exclaimed: "Nelly, my dear, if you don't put that kettle nearer the fire, it will never boil." I answered: "Oh yes it will, Ma. Just you listen, it will soon start to sing." She watched it intently until it began to sing and then to boil. Ma was amazed as I mashed the tea. Then she said: "I thought you said you were going to do us a bit of toast, my dear." I answered: "Yes, Ma. Watch that contraption in the middle of the table and it will do your toast." Ma was flabbergasted. "Well, I never," she repeated over and over again, but she was not too flabbergasted to eat an enormous pork-pie tea.

When it was time for them to go home, Ma put her arms around me, kissed and hugged me and said: "I have seen three wonderful things this afternoon: a kettle that boils without putting it on the fire, toast that had never even seen the fire, and the King and Queen of England, and I have had my tea here in the most beautiful room I have ever seen." Poor old Ma, she had not seen many nice rooms in her life, but it was a great compliment to my humble living-kitchen.

Another story concerns an old woman who came over one evening to watch television. ITV with its adverts had just started. When she saw the monkeys in the P.G. Tips advert, she exclaimed: "Well, I never! I really didn't know they could teach monkeys to speak for themselves. Now isn't that wonderful!" Poor old dear, we never disillusioned her.

One day during a bad storm our television aerial was struck by lightning, damaging the set beyond repair, so Sid and I travelled to Loughborough to choose a new one. When we came out of the shop, Sid bought a newspaper on a street corner. He stood reading it, then pointed to a figure, saying: "Nell, is that a one or a seven?" I thought it was a seven. Not feeling quite sure, he bought another paper. "Umm," he said, "it is a seven. I have just won £70 on a horse." "Oh jolly good," I said. "Add that £70 to the £90 I have saved, and we could buy the hide suite I have been wanting for years." "O.K.," answered Sid, "there's no time like the present. So off we went and bought a beautiful hide suite, guaranteed hide throughout, costing 140 guineas. When I was dusting it one day, I noticed that the back and sides felt colder than the rest so I upturned a chair, took out a few tacks and there found a selvedge. "Oh!" I thought, "hide throughout is it? This is the first cow ever to have grown a selvedge." I phoned and complained to the owner of the shop. He still maintained it was hide throughout, but when told about the selvedge, he said: "I'm on my way." He came and agreed to change the suite for one that was really and truly hide throughout.

Another old lady in her nineties lived in an old-world cottage opposite our farm. She was completely blind, but oh so wise! Whenever I was perplexed about my children's health, I had only to go across the road and this very old lady would give such good advice. She lived with her widowed daughter who had to go out to work to live. In those days she had only ten shillings a week widow's pension. As the old lady became increasingly infirm, her daughter became more and more worried at leaving her alone from 9 a.m. until 5 p.m., so I arranged with the old lady for her to disarrange her curtains if she needed help and I would go across immediately. Her white lace curtains always hung so immaculately that any disarrangement would be noticed. I had a habit every time I went out my back door to look across at these curtains. Only once were they disarranged, and that accidentally, but the time came when I was not happy without going across several times a day just to see if she was alright.

One day she was crying so heartbrokenly I said: "What is the matter, dear?" She told me her son had been to see her, he was suffering from cancer of the throat, and she could not understand what he was saying. His voice could not articulate what he had come to tell her, so he wrote it down on a paper. "My poor boy," she said to him, "I am blind, I cannot see to read your note." He left without her knowing what he wanted to tell her. The pathos of this story was enough to break their hearts.

She was always so brave and patient. When I went to see her, she would say: "It's Nelly." When I said: "How do you know it's me, dear?" she answered: "I can tell how you open the door, and I know your footsteps."

One day her daughter asked me to take her a drink, as she was not very well and was staying in bed. I took her a drink and found her daughter had left her some sandwiches beautifully cut so thinly and set on a tray with a perfectly ironed tray-cloth. How this daughter must have loved her old mother to set a tray so nicely even though she could not see it. She stayed in bed a few days, still saying when I entered her room: "It's Nelly."

Then the third day she said: "Who is it?" Then I knew she was dying. I told her daughter what had happened and that perhaps she should miss work for a while. She most readily agreed. It was only a few hours afterwards that she came across late that night to say her mother had died, and to ask what she could do. Sid fetched the undertaker, for in those days the village carpenter made the coffins, and he needed several days to do this work. Although I had never done it before, I helped wash the old lady and lay her out. She was ninety-two but she had the beautiful skin of a young girl. I missed the old lady, and also her daughter who bought a tiny cottage at the other end of the village, where she lived until she herself was well into her eighties. I never had quite such well-loved neighbours ever again.

In those days television programmes for children were very short. In any case, as they grew up, our twins started enjoying the fireside stories I made up for them. One cold winter evening we all sat before a huge fire. The twins sat one on each of my knees while Michael sat at my feet. Sid was reading his paper the other side of the fire, Sidney sat beside him reading a book, and David sat at the table doing his homework. The story that night was a good one, probably because I felt deeply happy. I had got well into the story when out of the corner of my eye I noticed Sid trying to listen, at the same time trying to read his newspaper. At last he put down his paper, drew his chair a little nearer the fire and settled down comfortably to listen to the story. Soon after, Sidney put down his book and also drew nearer the fire, looking quite interested in the story I was telling. This encouraged me to make the story more and more exciting. At long last David pushed his homework further up the table, and he, too, drew his chair into the circle around the fire. When I had finished the story, I looked around my family and said: "Well! did you all . enjoy that one?" All heartily agreed. Sid said to me: "Nell, I really believe you could make up a story about any mortal thing." I answered: "Do you know, Sid, I believe I could. Should we have a try? You start Sid. Choose something you think difficult." "Oh, dear!" says Sid, "I cannot think of anything." Just as he said this, three small lumps of coal fell off the fire. "Right," he said, "tell us a story about three lumps of coal that fell off a fire." This I immediately started to do: what the cook said to the lumps of coal, the squabble between the sauce-pans, the kettle trying to calm them down, the agreement they came to, and the meal they cooked for their family. Sid said: "I give up." The next challenge was: "Tell a story about this penny." "Oh!" I said, "That one is very easy. That penny went miles and miles in different people's pockets. It got lost a few times in various places, and eventually was the cause of a nice young man meeting a pretty girl, whom he eventually married." After that it was time for bed, but I had started something that snowballed. Every evening it was "Mummy, you couldn't possibly make up a story about this and that." At last I turned the tables on them by telling them that they in turn had to tell a story. We started with daddy. Oh dear, poor old Sid! He started like this: "Well, well, once

upon a time, um, oh . . . yes, once upon a time . . . " The children were looking at him expectantly and he was looking at me with a pleading look, so I whispered: "Yes, Sid, what about the calf that got a tin on its foot?" "Oh, yes," says Sid, much relieved, "that's it. Yes, once upon a time we had a calf and it got its foot in a tin and couldn't get it off. Yes, children, once upon a time we did have a calf who got a tin on its foot." Another imploring look at me. I whispered: "Tell them how you eventually got it off, Sid." The story went a bit better, then: how they got that tin off, how the foot bled, and how they bandaged it up. Then Sid was stuck again, so he finished the story saying: "And the calf lived happily ever after."

6

Bowls

WHEN our twins started school and were off our hands a bit, so to speak, Sid thought it was time I took up a game of some sort again. Tennis was my true sport, so I joined our village club once again, but found I had lost quite a lot of the energy needed for that game, so after a lot of persuasion from Sid, I set myself up with a brand new set of woods and joined the Wymeswold Ladies Bowls Club. To tell the truth, I had always looked on lawn bowls as an old man's game but, like many others before me, I was astounded at the skill needed by a first-class bowler and at the terrific fascination that takes hold of players, once they have started to play in matches and competitions. Sid had played the game for many years, proving himself among the best players. He was very determined to make me a good bowler, too, taking me down to the green to practise at every available opportunity. He even bought me a book written by a world-renowned champion which helped me a great deal to understand many of the finer points. In a short time they put me in matches, and I was hooked for the rest of my life by this marvellous game, surprising myself at the way I so quickly learned the rules. But there! Sid was a patient and very good teacher. Before my first season was over, I was skipping a rink in all our matches.

I became just as enamoured of bowls as Sid was, so much so we went to Skegness twice every year to play in tournaments. Playing together in the pairs, we reached the finals several times, but never won. One year in the open singles, in which there were over 2000 entries, Sid reached the last eight, and I reached the last sixteen, being knocked out by the only other lady left in the tournament. That same year, on Ladies' Day, I reached the final, and after leading six shots to nothing was pipped at the post by a Skegness lady. During an earlier round I had beaten the previous year's winner of the beautiful Rose Bowl. She only scored one shot. I was told she was so upset she went into the toilet to have a good cry.

During some of the early rounds in the open singles I met and beat many champions. I was once drawn to play against the Nottingham champion of champions, although I did not discover this until after the game. I beat him by one shot, after having tied, then needing to play an extra end, which I luckily won. In one round my opponent, who only scored four shots, said to me: "I'm not a fool you know." I asked him: "What makes you say that?" He answered: "You are playing so well, you make me look like one." He then told me that a few weeks before he had skipped a triples rink in the Bournemouth tournament and won it.

During the later stages of this particular tournament I came up against a Skegness doctor whom we had known by sight for many years but had never really met, either on or off the green. Now when I play bowls, competitive or friendly, I am a right chatterbox, but this doctor never spoke a word. I began to feel he thought himself much superior to me, so I shut up, and set about trying to beat him. I concentrated so hard that he only scored four shots. Much to my surprise, after I had beaten him so soundly, he shook me warmly by the hand, congratulating me on my performance through this tournament. When we walked off the green, the doctor's friend came up to tell me how well I had played. After quite a friendly conversation I told him how puzzled I had been that his friend had not spoken one word during our game. He then told me he and his doctor friend had watched me play at Skegness for many years, and when he had to play me in this tournament, he was so scared he trembled and just could not talk to me. "Good gracious me!" I said. I did not know whether to take this as a compliment or not. However, we got on very well during the rest of that glorious week's bowling.

I became so dedicated to this game that, after winning our village championship cup several times, my name was sent up for consideration for the county team.

I was picked first as a number two, but afterwards I skipped a rink. Several of my younger children told me years afterwards how they got sick and tired to death of bowls. They said: "We had bowls for breakfast, bowls for dinner and bowls for tea." The one who slept in the bedroom next to ours told the others: "You're lucky. I have bowls after I get to bed. Mummy and daddy talk nothing else after they come to bed, and I cannot sleep." Bless the kids, they were much too kind to hurt our feelings by telling us we were overdoing bowls a bit. I must admit that each meal we lived over again our last game. The salt pot took the place of the jack, and other bits and pieces were placed to illustrate just how the woods were drawn to the jack.

I remember when I was president of our village ladies' club, telling the players just how much I enjoyed the game. In fact, I sometimes enjoyed the same game three times over. First the actual game when played, secondly telling Sid all about how the ends went, and thirdly I would quite often dream about that same game.

I hope that I do not sound as if I am boasting about my prowess at bowls, for on reading this over it sounds quite a bit like it. Which reminds me of that year I did so well on ladies' day at Skegness. I was late for every meal. The other guests, most of whom were bowlers, fired questions at me: "Are you still in? Who did you beat last? Who do you play in the next round?" Of course, in my excitement at reaching the finals I overelaborated my explanations, until I thought: "Golly, woman, quieten down a bit!" I apologized for what sounded like blowing my own trumpet by saying: "Sorry, this sounds like boasting." Then a quiet voice from a gentleman sitting on the other side of the dining room said: "Not boasting, Mrs Smith, only a little overenthusiastic. Carry on, I love to hear it." I could have hugged him, for I really had started to feel embarrassed by my own chatter.

An amusing game took place at Skegness one year in a very early round of the pairs. Sid and I, who were in our late fifties, were playing two ladies who were both in their seventies. Early in the game these two ladies complained of feeling ill, so Sid, being the gentleman he was, said: "Nell, don't throw a long jack. If we cannot beat these old dears on short jacks, we will go out." Which is just what we did. There was Sid picking up their woods and handing them to save them bending. We were three parts through the game before we realized their cunning, far too late to pull ourselves together to win the game. We came off the green laughing our heads off, and were met by other players who had lost to these two old dears using the same technique. We watched the two ladies reach the final of the pairs, the winners of which had no qualms as regards their opponents, having been warned by several previous losers.

I remember how, in the early years of my bowling, I picked up another person's woods which looked exactly like mine, including the initials E.S. In the next match, when I started to play, I realized these bowls were much too heavy. I examined them and found they did not pair up exactly with my other two. I got in touch with the clubs we had recently played, but with no luck. Then at the end of that season, we were playing at Kegworth and I noticed this pair of woods just like mine. I picked one up and examined it against the woods I was playing with, and I knew they were mine. I jumped a foot into the air shouting: "I've found my woods, I've found my woods," when a man's sour voice shouted: "What do you mean you've found your woods. They are my woods." "Oh no!" I answered, "these are my woods, yours are sitting in the boot of that car. Just you go and look." This man had played with my woods all through the season, not realizing they were not his own. Needless to say, I was delighted to have a complete set of woods once again.

One of the best tournaments Sid and I ever enjoyed was the Ashby pairs, which took three days to complete. One year Sid and I reached the finals. Only once before had a lady reached the final, and never had a lady won it. We had a specially good pair to face in this final: two miners renowned for winning pairs tournaments. I was so excited, all the

Ashby ladies were rooting for us. On the twenty-first end we tied. It was my turn for the jack. The other lead was visibly trembling. After Sid had bowled his last wood, we lay four and the end looked like this:

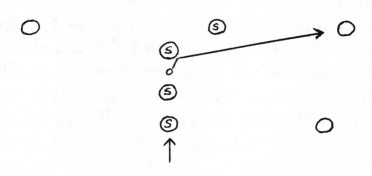

With his last wood the opposing skip hit my front wood, which hit our second wood, which drove the jack onto our third wood and then out to one of their side woods. Never did such a bad wood deserve less to be shot and to win a final. A groan went through the spectators.

Joining the village bowls club brought many other pleasures, such as what we called the bowls supper. Sometimes this was held in the village hall, the ladies of the club doing the catering, but occasionally the menfolk suggested we go out, to enable the ladies to enjoy a night out without any responsibility.

I especially remember one dinner we had at the Yew Tree Inn at Kegworth. The Wymeswold club had invited many members from other clubs. We had a slap-up dinner followed by a social. Sid and I were asked to do a skit on Cynthia and Hilda Baker. We had done a similar one once before on a wet President's Day when play was rained off. I gave this a lot of thought, as Hilda had all the talking to do, and Sid, as Cynthia, was just a stooge. I thought up the script in bed, long after Sid was asleep. (I did a lot of thinking in bed instead of going to sleep.) I started the skit by dressing up Sid in a lady bowler's outfit, which proved hilarious before a word was spoken. I had pleated yards of white calico into a wrap-round skirt. None of our lady bowlers were big enough to own a skirt the size my Sid needed, but one did have a white cardigan which had stretched so much in the washing machine that it hung loosely even on Sid. To crown all, we borrowed a funny little hat which had shrunk rather badly and stuck on Sid's head like a tom-tit on a roof. In the skit Cynthia and Hilda had been chosen to play for their county, and were sitting on a village green seat waiting to be picked up by the bus which was a long time coming. To pass the time, Hilda was finding faults in a number of men bowlers who were visitors at the dinner, but calling them by ladies names. Jack became Jackaline, John Joan, Joe Josephine, Will Wilhelmina, but everyone knew exactly who the dart was being thrown at. Sid kept up the laughter by taking out of his handbag a lipstick and mirror, making a horrible mess of his lips. Then he pretended to go to sleep. I started to sing to the tune of "Where have all the flowers gone?", substituting "Where oh where has our bus gone, long time coming." Suddenly I woke up Cynthia and asked her if she still had the ticket from the County. She handed it to me, but on looking at it, we found the date for the match was the day before. We finished by Cynthia being chased off the stage by the angry Hilda Baker.

One of the gentlemen visitors told me

how he had enjoyed the skit, saying he had laughed until it hurt. "My! Missus," he exclaimed, "you and Sid must have rehearsed that lot a great many times." "No," I answered, "we haven't rehearsed it once." He laughed derisively, saying: "I just don't believe you." "Right," I said, and challenged him to ask Sid the same question, to see if he would get the same answer. Still not believing me, he strutted across the room to Sid, whose answer to his query was the same as mine. "You see," Sid said, "I didn't have to speak a word. That was all left to Nell. And you know what a chatterbox she is. No trouble at all to her." At last he believed us.

Belonging to a bowls club, one meets many people, making friendships which last a lifetime. Those who jeer at bowls as just an old man's game should think twice because they do not know what they are missing. Most of my family love the game. As my sons grew older, we were able to raise a rink of four — Sid, Sidney, Richard and myself. When David came home from Canada we had five.

All my sons have been good at

sport. Sidney played badminton for his county, David played badminton for his university, and both Sidney and his son Marcus played bowls for their county, as did Sid and I.

7

Sadness, Tiffs and a Trip to Paris

OUR family had been so wonderfully happy, but as happens in all families, a sad time was coming. Sadly, father suffered a stroke which left him partially paralysed. This meant he needed constant nursing. My mother and sister Lottie managed through the day, but the rest of the family took it in turns to do the night duty. Even Edna, who was a nurse living in London, spent her holidays at home. She said she wanted to give the others a rest, never thinking that she was not giving herself a rest. My father lived three years with home nursing like this. Sometimes it was extremely difficult for me to help. One instance was when my twins were ill. They both had a high temperature and it was my night on duty with father. Sid kept saying: "We will be alright, Nell, I'll look after the twins." I was still worried.

Sid was such a heavy sleeper. I kept thinking: "Would he hear them?" At last I started the long walk to my parents' house. I got well on the way when I felt I just could not leave my twins. I turned back, and when I reached our farm gate, stood thinking a while, then decided the twins had got their daddy, and my dad needed me badly, so I turned around again and spent the night with Dad. Fortunately the twins were a bit better the next morning.

Not only was father ill, Sid's favourite Aunt Nan also suffered a stroke, a much worse one than father's. We looked after her for one week, then her husband decided she must go into hospital where she died a few days afterward. There is an old saying: it never rains but it pours, or rather troubles never come singly. Father and Aunt Nan died, and my brother John lost his wife Sally, all in the space of a few years.

But the worst shock to all our families was when Kath's stepson Michael rang us one Sunday morning to tell us that his father had just died of a heart attack. Sid and I rushed down to Loughborough to be with Kath in this time of loss. Kath was stunned that, after only eleven years of a supremely happy marriage, Vin was taken away from her so suddenly. After a while she sold her house, and my brothers built her a bungalow in Wymeswold. While they built the bungalow, Kath and her young son Robert came to live with us at the farm. I like to think that our family helped Kath and Robert to recover from such a terrible blow. Kath is such a good person. This second sudden loss did not seem fair, but after she moved into her new bungalow, she bravely set about bringing up her son in the best possible way. She was offered a teaching job, but she preferred staying home with Robert, wanting him to have the benefit of a mother at home when he arrived home from school. Wymeswold residents were lucky to have Kath back again in our village, as she did a tremendous amount of social work. Many people were grateful for her help and kindness. I myself received much love and help from her, which I shall never forget.

Sidney and Mary down at Clay House Farm had two sons, Kevin, the firstborn, and Marcus. Later on a daughter was born whom they named Gaynor. By this time our David had gained his Bachelor of Arts degree and was doing teaching and research in Paris. He very much hoped that Sid and I would spend a week in Paris with him. We decided to do this and make it our holiday for that year.

We had just bought a new car, so we travelled in leisurely fashion down to Newhaven. On the way Sid and I had one of our extremely rare quarrels. I had driven the car as far as Eton, where I stopped at some lights. I did not know which way to turn, and I let the lights change without moving. Sid got exasperated. I beckoned the traffic behind me to go past, but the lorry driver behind me shouted: "Get cracking, Missus, I canna climb over yer." I got cracking but certainly on the wrong road. Sid was really furious with me, more so than I thought I deserved. I had driven all those miles without advice from anyone, which was quite good for a countrywoman not used to driving long distances. Road signs had been taken down during the war and were very few and far between, unlike the well-posted roads of today. Sid kept nagging about my silly mistake at the lights, so I stopped the car on a quiet bit of road and invited Sid into the driving seat, saying: "I have driven the longest half of the journey. Now you do the other half. But don't ask me the way, find it for yourself." Although I knew I was in the wrong, I felt quite hurt at the way Sid had chastised me.

He calmly slid into the driver's seat, but it was not long before I knew he had taken a wrong turning. I was much too huffy to tell him so, but he kept on for about eight miles before he said: "I have a feeling, Nell, we are going the wrong way." I did not answer, as I was still feeling hard done by, so Sid stopped the car on the side of the road, looked straight at me with such an appealing look, and said: "Don't be like this, Nell. It's not like us." Of course, it ended in a clinch, both of us glad to be on normal terms again. What passers-by thought of two middle-aged people hugging each other in broad daylight, we neither knew nor cared. We then studied the map and found we were well out of our way, but it did not matter in the least. We were together again and we had all day to finish our journey.

Sid and I rarely quarrelled, but I can think of one or two silly, or even amusing disagreements. We had only been married a few weeks when he asked me to mend his old working jacket. "Oh dear, Sid," I said, "that coat is more holes than material." "Hmm," he answered, "that's just what me mum said, and she wouldn't do it. But I thought you might, being a dressmaker." I answered: "Well, I shan't. I could make a new dress in the time it would take to darn all those tears you've made while hedge cutting." "Oh, alright," says Sid, "I'll do it myself." This he proceeded to do with the help of a huge darning needle and pieces of old wool. I kept giving his work a surreptitious look, feeling more and more worried. I thought: "People will think I have mended that jacket." At last I could stand it no longer. I said: "Give it to me. I'll do my best to make it respectable." He thankfully gave me the coat which took several evenings to finish, but I made a real good job of it, partly because it was a labour of love. His mother said: "Nellie, you are a Trojan to mend that jacket. It really wasn't worth it." I answered: "I really couldn't let Sid wear a coat botched and codged like he started to do it." And I had been obliged to undo his work before I could start. When Sid put on his coat, he kissed and hugged me saying: "Thanks, Nell, I knew you would do it rather than let people see my handiwork."

Another time we quarrelled was when I had decorated our sitting room, and I wanted a couple of nails hammering into the wall to hang a pair of pictures. Now Sid and I were never handymen. I was, and still am, absolutely hopeless with a hammer and nails. To start with he got a six-inch nail — to find the joint between the bricks, he said. I watched horror-struck as he kept hammering hole after hole, spoiling my new wallpaper. "Stop it," I shouted, "I'll get someone to do it who knows his job." Afterwards I learned one could buy a proper little hook, with three wee nails that held a picture securely.

Let me get back to our trip to Paris. We arrived at Newhaven around four o'clock, where we parked our car for one week, then asked around about lodgings for the night. At last we found a retired couple who took visitors for bed and breakfast. We enjoyed a chat with this grand old couple before going to bed, and looked forward to seeing them on our return from Paris. Our trip across the English Channel was most enjoyable. We both proved good sailors, as neither of us felt sick. We also enjoyed a good dinner. We arrived at Dieppe and there took a train for Paris. The thing that surprised me most was the number of small farmhouses. One could not tell which was the farmhouse and which were the outbuildings, that is until one found a chimney, which was the only clue. On seeing these dreadfully poor farms, I had a sense of pleasure when I thought of our lovely farmhouse with its spacious rooms, placed well away from the farm buildings.

David met us at the station and took us to our hotel. We were taken to our large room serving as a sitting and bedroom, with one small room with a toilet and washbowl. The first morning we found this washbowl half full of filthy water, a backwash from the pipes. One could not possibly have a wash, so I went back to bed and picked up the phone to talk to the management, who were supposed to be able to speak English. I explained slowly and distinctly about the trouble with the washbowl. The answer I got was: "Thank you, yes, egg and bacon for two." I cried out: "No! No!", then went through it all again even more slowly, but still the answer was: "Thank you, yes, egg and bacon for two." I gave up. We enjoyed our egg and bacon for two, then slid down the bed again until David came to our rescue around ten o'clock. He saw our trouble and went to speak to the manager who immediately came and put the bowl right. Apparently they often had this trouble.

David took us to see most of the sights of Paris. We were much impressed by the width of their roads, much wider than our London roads. We did not like the oily foods. Sid said on our last day there that he could not eat another French meal, so we bought some of their lovely bread, half a pound of butter, and a pound of cooked ham. This we secreted into David's room at the university residence where he boiled a small saucepan of water and made us tea. This was not allowed in the students' rooms, so we had to make quite sure we did not leave any crumbs as evidence. Sid gave a great sigh of contentment, saying: "That's the best meal I have had since we came to Paris."

We visited a night club called the Moulin Rouge. A policeman on duty outside talked to David. The gist of the message was: "Don't go in there. They don't charge much entrance fee, but my, don't they sting inside!" We soon found that was only too true. David ordered four glasses of port wine. The staggering cost of these four glasses was 25 shillings each glass, an awful lot of money in those days. David said: "Gracious! I haven't got enough money to pay for that lot. Have you Dad?" We found enough between us and paid up. Needless to say that one glass each had to last us all night. It was an expensive experience and one that I would not want to repeat.

We went to a couple of race meetings, one with David at Longchamps, the other at Maisons-Lafitte. As David was teaching on this second occasion, we were supposed to meet his friend on a certain platform of a certain underground station. But we got out at the wrong one, so of course David's friend was not there to meet us. Oh dear! We waited, wondering what had happened to him, until time was getting short. Sid was determined to go to these races, so we left the station, racing up the steps to the street, where Sid hailed a taxi. Then, not speaking much French, we could not make the driver understand where we wanted to go. The taxi was on the point of driving away, when Sid had the sudden thought of miming a man on horseback whipping his horse. Immediately the driver understood, exclaiming "I understand" and motioned us to get in. We did not really know if he had understood, but eventually we arrived at our destination where fortunately we soon found David's friend, thanks to his great height. David was six feet three inches, his friend taller still. Sid enjoyed the races much more than I. The smell of garlic from the people in those stands was horrible. Our clothes smelt of garlic weeks after we returned home.

David asked us if we would take a case of his books home, but we did a silly thing. I thought Sid had the key to the case, he thought I had, but no, we had left it in David's room. On going through customs we found out our mistake. I suggested to the customs officer that they keep the case of books until we could obtain the key from David in France. "Oh," he said, "go on. I'll trust you." He looked through our other cases but found nothing suspicious and let us through.

On the return journey our boat was overcrowded in second class. Sid and I were among the lucky ones who were put in first-class cabins to ease the pressure on second class. It was a lovely cabin, fitted out in silver grey and a very pale wine shade. The colours went beautifully together. When the waiter asked Sid if he would like the French or the English meal, Sid answered: "English, of course, and thank God you have an English meal, for I really couldn't face another of those oily garlic meals."

On our return to Newhaven we again stayed with that grand old couple who had been so kind to us. After a perfectly cooked meal, we went out for an evening walk. Then we rang up home to tell them we had arrived in Newhaven, but we were going to spend a few days visiting some of the south-coast towns.

Sidney answered the phone and, just at the end of the conversation, suddenly said: "We have a huge shock for you when you arrive home, mother." When I asked what kind of a shock, he said: "I'm not telling you until you are home." I pleaded with him to tell me, as neither of us would have had a wink of sleep thinking whatever had happened. He still said: "No, I won't tell you." "Right," I said, coming the heavy parent stuff. "I'll keep ringing you until you tell us, and I really mean this, I shall." After this threat, he told us that our farm was up for sale.

8

Purchase of our Farm

TRINITY COLLEGE Cambridge was selling the Wymeswold estate to provide money to build new halls of residence. They had taken photos of all the farm houses to illustrate their catalogue. The farms were advertised to be sold by auction a month later. Sid and I were absolutely stunned. We had visions of our farms being sold to the highest bidder, and of our being, if not actually turned out, made so uncomfortable that we would not want to stay. We thought it was a dreadful thing to do to tenants whose families had farmed the same land for generations. Of course, we went straight home the next day, after having an absolutely sleepless night.

On our arrival home we met some of the other tenant farmers who were just as worried as we were. For a fortnight this news was like a blight on our village life. It affected so many families as well as the farmers. In those days many of the Wymeswold men worked on the farms. My own feelings were deeply affected. At last I took the bull by the horns and wrote a long letter to the bursar of Trinity College. I poured out the hurt the farmers were suffering at their farms being put up for auction, without their first being given the chance to buy them. I had the temerity to ask him outright if he thought Trinity College was acting fairly to farmers who had always paid the rent when due, who for the most part had farmed the land well, and whose families had been tenants for several generations.

When the bursar received my letter, the agents were sent straight up to Wymeswold. They asked all the farmers if they would like to buy their farms. Everyone said they did, if the price was within their means. No price was mentioned at that first meeting. The agents had been sent to sound out the wishes of the farmers, and we were told we would be hearing from Trinity in due course. Then followed the anxious time of waiting. Would we be offered the first chance of our farms, or would they still go up for auction? The relief was tremendous when we learned that Trinity wanted £42,000 for the whole estate, including the old schoolmaster's house and a cottage rented by an old lady named Miss Morris. These two and all the farmers were told that they all had to agree, so that everything could be sold at once, otherwise they were to go up for auction, as the college did not want any one piece left on its hands.

A meeting was called which all the farmers attended, but not the two with houses only. A lengthy meeting was held where everything was discussed apart from getting an agreement as regards the £42,000. A second meeting was called, but there again nothing concrete was attained. I had attended both these meetings without saying a word but at the third meeting which looked like ending the same way, I asked if I might make a suggestion. The chairman, one of the farmers called Bob Mills, said: "Please do, Mrs Smith. Perhaps a woman's suggestion might break the deadlock." I started by saying that, if we bought our farms, all the money I possessed would have to be used, and that gave me a certain right to say what I thought we should do. I looked at the chairman, who like everyone else had the catalogue of the sale in his hands. I said: "Mr Mills, you are the tenant of the largest farm and first in the catalogue. If you and then all the other tenants in their turn stated purely and simply how much they would give for their land, then we could add it all together and see how near we were to Trinity's asking price. But," I warned, "don't anyone state a silly price, or we shall get nowhere." I also said: "Deep down we all know exactly how far we can go."

Mr Mills said: "Mrs Smith, that is the best suggestion yet." He stated how much he would go up to per acre. Sid was the one who wrote it all down on paper as he was an excellent man with figures. They went through the whole catalogue, each farmer stating a fair price for his land. When Sid reckoned up all the acres at the different prices, it came within range of Trinity's asking price. However, Trinity refused this first offer, so the farmers met again and arrived at a revised figure. To be exact, the sum amounted to £40,000, without the two houses whose tenants refused to attend the meetings. We all thought this was a satisfactory effort, so the next suggestion was to ring Trinity and put this offer. Sid was the one voted to be the speaker on the phone. The answer was disappointing: the bursar was at a dinner and we were to ring again in an hour's time. That hour was so long, we were all in a state of trauma, except Sid, and he seemed as cool as a cucumber. When the hour was up, Sid grinned, and said: "Here goes." After a short wait, which seemed an awful long one, Sid started to tell the decision we had reached: to offer £40,000. The answer was: "We must have the £42,000." Now Sid took the bull by the horns and said it had taken us three whole evenings to reach our figure, and that he thought £40,000 plus a house and cottage was quite an achievement. He said that if they could not accept this figure, they would have to put the farms up for auction. We others in the room were aghast at his temerity in saying this without further discussion with the rest of the farmers, but we all faintly heard the answer to this threat at the other end of the wire: "Wait a minute, Mr Smith. Don't be so hasty. We will have a little discussion at this end." They had their discussion, decided to sell the farms for that figure, and told us the agents would be up the following day with the agreements to sign.

Everyone breathed a sigh of relief, until the next morning when two farmers, who were tenants for only a few acres each, revoked. This put everyone in a quandary. Trinity would not sell to us without these two who had only thirty odd acres between them. I raced round to the other farmers suggesting that the rest of us should form a consortium and buy these acres between us, although we were already stretched to the limit without this added amount. We all agreed to do this, and I went to tell these two just what we had decided. Perhaps they did not like the idea of our being their landlords. At any rate they changed their minds and decided to stick with their bargain. The agreements were signed, and then came the worst thing: finding the money to pay for the farms. For us it was particularly hard. Sidney had only been a tenant farmer for a few years and had not saved much in that short time. By pooling everything we had and Sidney obtaining a mortgage on the farm we managed to find the money.

Some time before buying the farm, I had received a letter from an old man named Mr Crosland from whom I had previously bought a caravan. He offered me the chance to buy his bungalow that stood in around two acres of ground. He was getting old, he said, and was going to live with a relative. After much bargaining I bought this very attractive little place, with the idea of renovating the bungalow myself, and Sid and Sidney putting the large garden and paddock in better order, then selling it. How fortunate we were in putting it up for auction, for we made a good profit. This money was a great help when paying for the farms.

I often wonder if Trinity College ever

regretted selling the Wymeswold estate to build new halls of residence. Our recently modernised farmhouse alone would be worth the money paid for the whole estate, while all those hundreds of acres are worth at least £1800 per acre. It seems incredible that prices have risen so much in less than thirty years.

After the excitement and thrill of buying our farms, both Sidney and Mary and ourselves settled down to really hard slogging. Wherever we could save a shilling, we saved, and wherever we could make an extra shilling, so we did, but after a few years, having no rent to pay, we began to recover our financial position, to enjoy a better standard of living, and even to buy more land to add to our farms. The pride that we felt when taking an evening stroll round our land was indescribable. The joy it gave us to discuss the different crops and watch the animals, all of which we owned ourselves, without owing a penny to anyone!

In due time our thoughts began to turn to buying a brand-new combine harvester. In our early farming years the corn was thrashed by the travelling steam-driven threshing machine. Then later we bought a threshing drum which was powered by the tractor. But now we owned two farms with over two hundred acres, Sidney and his dad decided in 1963 to launch out on a combine harvester.

How right they were. The harvest from both farms was gathered in an incredibly short time. Electric drying machines were installed, which did the work that we used to have to wait for the sun to do. Corn stacks gradually became a thing of the past, and a new baler was bought which lifted up and pressed the straw into tight and tidy bales, fastening them safely with binder twine ready for stacking under our new dutch barn. Sidney's farm was already equipped with a number of these barns. Other modern machines were bought to help in the haymaking, such as hay turners and balers.

We grew many less acres of root crops such as mangolds and turnips. In their place silage was made, lessening the back-breaking job of lifting and cleaning each root, then carting them to the farm for clamping. The cows seemed to love this horrible-smelling silage, and milked equally well on it as they did when eating the mangolds and turnips.

All the new machines were so efficient that many farm labourers were made redundant. In our first years of farming, one would see a dozen or more men clearing a field of corn sheaves, lifting them on to carts ready for their journey to the stackyard. The lovely sight of these heavy loads of corn drawn by those strong shire horses is sadly a thing of the past. A team of eleven men, all specialists in their appointed work, was needed to do the threshing. These days a combine harvester needs one man to drive the machine, with a follow-up of a tractor and trailer to take home the corn. In our young days we could not possibly have envisaged the rapid change that would take place in farming after World War II.

9

New Poultry Venture

ONE day an animal food representative for one of the big firms had a long chat with us about setting up a broiler house. He explained that his firm would help in financing this venture if we agreed to use their poultry meal for the next five years. The building to hold five thousand birds would cost £2,500. We were very interested in this new venture, but did not like the idea of being tied to one food firm for five years. We told him we would discuss this matter together and tell him our decision the next time he came. We decided to erect the building immediately. When it was up, I thought it looked huge. It certainly was at that time, but now there are buildings for that purpose five times the size. We paid for it ourselves, so as not to be beholden to the feed firm. Electric strip lighting was installed, but the heating arrangements consisted of four huge hoovers fed by propane gas. Electric heating was rejected because of the danger of power failures, which in severe weather definitely would cause the young chicks death within only a matter of fifteen minutes. While we were rearing our first batch of five thousand chicks, an experienced poultry farmer said to us: "You just about need to live wi' 'em the first few days." Our first batch of broilers paid us a handsome profit of £400.

We sent our birds to a firm at Melton Mowbray for killing and preparing for the table. These birds went in two batches on the same day, the same lorry fetching them. The empty lorry and crates went over a weighbridge before fetching the birds, then again with the loaded birds. The time came when Sid was very dissatisfied with the weight of the second load. He was so upset he demanded that this load be weighed again with him watching. He was proved so right. Had he not insisted on their being weighed again, he would have lost £112 on that one load. After that, one of us always followed the loaded birds in our car to make sure they were weighed correctly, with all four wheels on the weighbridge. On farms there are so many ways in which dishonesty can take place. For instance, even with reputable firms a lorry driver can leave several bags of food short. We were very trustful people, and it was not until we realized this was happening during the war that we started to count the bags of food before signing for them.

That poultry house was the start of an enterprise that grew beyond our wildest dreams. For a few years the broiler business boomed. Then so many farmers entered into the same business that we started to lose money because of over-production. We were beginning to think our great broiler house would become a white elephant — the work and expense entailed was bringing in only a pittance — when Bob, who was still working for us, said he had seen advertised a large battery house, including the cages, which had had only two batches of laying hens through it. Sid wondered about gradually selling our free-range birds and poultry houses, and buying this huge battery house, so we went to inspect this building in a village eight miles away. Egg production had always been one of Sid's favourite occupations. He thought he could raise the chicks in the broiler house, then move then into their battery house as twenty-week-old pullets. This enterprise took a long time to decide, but at last we bought the battery house for £1,500 and it was placed on a concrete floor, two fields away from our farm house. Included was a huge food store and an egg-room with electric fans to help control the environment. The house held two thousand laying hens which laid nearly two thousand eggs each day during their peak laying period. It was so exciting, gathering as many eggs in an hour as it took three or four hours to gather from free range hens.

At first I was extremely dubious about keeping caged birds. I wondered if it would be cruel to the birds. But after a time I realized that, if they were well fed and always had water before them, they were quite as happy as our free-range birds. In fact, in certain extreme weathers they were much better off. In winter free-range birds are extremely miserable. They do not mind the cold, but they hate rain and wind. In frosty weather I have seen our birds walking as though on stilts. They paddle in the wet parts around their hut and the mud freezes on their feet and they make a miserable clucking sound. Often when I had finished my free-range round, hands and feet frozen, I stepped thankfully into our warm battery house. The birds welcomed you with their happy chirping.

An experienced poultry farmer knows all the different sounds his birds make. There is their hungry sound, quite a demanding sound, then the lovely contented sound when they are tucking into their new lot of meal. Then there is a sound of fright, quite a panicky sound, when something unusual happens, like a loud bang, or a rat entering the house, or even a dog. I get my birds used to the dogs and cats by letting them in regularly. Then, like free-range birds, they go hysterical if something really frightens them badly, like a noisy low-flying plane. When anything like that happens in our battery houses, I walk around singing at the top of my voice. Within seconds the birds quieten down, and start a kind of singing noise back to me. This has to be seen and heard to be believed. Many of my friends have scoffed at me when I have told them my birds sing back to me. Then I have taken them into the battery house, banged on something to make a noise which starts the birds off with their panicky noise, then opened the door and started my loud singing. Soon my birds prove me right, much to my friends' surprise and delight. I tell them my birds know the Londonderry Air as well as I know it myself. I sing to them as I gather their eggs, one of my helpers, Susan Jalland, whistles to them and they love it. A happy contented bird returns your care of them by laying many more eggs than an uncared-for flock, or even a free-range bird at its best in good weather. We were so happy about battery hens that we sold our free-range birds and all their houses, putting them up for auction. We had a good sale: both the huts and birds fetched good prices.

We settled down to producing these

eggs, but egg prices were so bad we did not make much money from them, until a wonderful thing happened. Our twin son Richard was going on a youth hostel holiday, and had ordered an extra large duffel bag to be made specially to the size he needed. On the Friday night, before starting his holiday, he went to Loughborough to fetch his duffel bag. To his chagrin the man had not finished it. He told Richard to go back on the Saturday morning at eight o'clock and it would be finished in time for his meeting with his friends. On Saturday morning his father took him down for eight o'clock, but the bag was not quite finished, so Richard sat with the man watching him work on it, while Sid had a walk around the market. Nearly everything imaginable was being sold, but Sid noticed there was not an egg stall. He mentioned this to one of the stall holders, saying he would love to start a market stall selling home-produced eggs. The man said: "Why don't you go to the town hall and see the market manager? You might stand a chance." This he did and was promised there might be a chance, as there was no egg stall and he liked to balance his market stalls. He told Sid he would let him know after the meeting of the people who decided these things.

The first week in September 1965 we were on our way to Skegness for a week's holiday when we met the postman who handed us our letters. We popped them in the glove compartment and forgot about them until we arrived at our destination. On opening our letter we learned that Sid was asked to attend a meeting the following Thursday about obtaining a market stall. Sid immediately sent a letter apologizing for not attending the Thursday meeting, but asked if he could attend their next meeting. On our return home a letter was waiting for us from Mr Green, the market manager, in which Sid was asked to attend their meeting the following Thursday. We were quite excited to learn we had been allocated a small stall, only six feet in length, every other Saturday. This was called a casual stall. The first Saturday we took in only £27, but each Saturday we improved on that figure. After a few weeks, Mr Green

informed us that we were to have another stall every other Saturday, but only until one o'clock. This was a much larger stall let to a jeweller every week, but he did not use it until one o'clock. We gladly took advantage of having this opportunity to sell our eggs each week, but we found great difficulty in vacating our stall by one o'clock, often having a queue at that time waiting to be served eggs.

We were getting much better known, as customers told their friends that our eggs really were fresh. Mr Green could see our great difficulty in leaving a queue of customers not served, so it was to our real delight that he told us we had been allocated a large stall every week at the same spot. This was a tremendous help. The stall was well placed for easy unloading of eggs and for attracting customers. From the time we obtained this new stall we went from strength to strength. We soon realized that we would have to enlarge our flock from 2000 to 3500 birds. We therefore had to build new accommodation for these extra birds, and do it quickly too, else we should be refusing good customers.

We bought another 1300 chicks to be housed at the age of twenty weeks.

Just after we had extended so much, Sid was taken seriously ill with sciatica, which was so bad it necessitated a period of three months in bed. This meant I had to manage the market stall by myself. Sid had been driving the eggs to market in a new Land Rover, which we found most unsuitable for the confined spaces we had to negotiate. He hated the thought of my driving this huge four-wheel-drive vehicle in such difficult circumstances, so we sold the Land Rover and bought a new Bedford van, which was easy to drive, and had a much better lock, which enabled me to get into and through almost impossible places. The market people I found very helpful: when I was in a tight corner, there was always a stall holder to help me through this congested market. Quite often I had only an inch or so to spare on each side of the van.

I remember once some stall holders, however, were not so cooperative. The van had to mount the curb and, when easing off again, it caught an old car belonging to another stall holder, who had parked it badly, leaving very little room for others to pass. I could hardly see the scratch it made, and it was such an old battered car I never gave it a thought that he might make a claim on me, especially as he had caused the obstruction by parking so badly. But the next Saturday he confronted me and said he had got a price for respraying the side of his car, and I would have to pay £25. I told him: "Not on your life will I pay anything like £25. The scratch my van made is minute at the side of all the knocks and bangs your car has received during its long life. Do you really expect me to pay for the wear and tear of years? Well, I shall not!" He became angry and asked for the name of our insurance firm, which I gave him. When I rang the insurance and told them the circumstances, they advised me to pay him £10 to get him off my back, but to get a letter from him stating he would make no further claim. This went against the grain with me — in those days £10 took a lot of earning — but Sid said I was to give him the £10 and forget it.

It was amusing to find myself in

exactly the same position a few weeks later — no room to manipulate my van because he had taken more than his share of parking space. He beckoned me on through an impossibly narrow space. I refused and called to him: "You must move. I will not try to get through, as I shall touch your car again, and then you will want another £10." "What!" shouted another stall holder. "Did you really give him £10 for that tiny scratch? More fool you! That bugger makes more out of his blasted car being bumped than ever he makes on his stall." So afterwards I reported him to the market manager for his bad parking, making it so difficult for everyone else. The manager said I was one of many to report him, and this time he had just got to park fairly.

We have had our difficulties with our market stall. One dark winter morning the roads were covered with snow and frost and, to make matters worse, a fresh lot of snow had fallen during the night, covering all traces of tracks and bad parts in the road. We were the first vehicle out on the road which in the dark made keeping to the road very hazardous. I managed very well for a couple of miles, when I thought I was leaving the middle of the road. I swerved to the left, but found myself in a deep trench dug in the grass at the side of the road. I managed to keep the engine going and crept out, leaving part of the exhaust in the trench, and dozens of smashed eggs in the van. What a mess! But I did not worry unduly, because we managed to limp to market, making a dreadful noise, loud enough to wake the dead. At least we did not disappoint our customers by not being there.

Never once in nearly eighteen years have we missed going to our market stall, but once, and only once in all those years, did we break down. This was a traumatic experience. I had bought a new Commer van with a diesel engine, and during one of the coldest times on record, the diesel froze after we had covered only one mile of our journey. That morning I had been so pleased to hear the engine start first pull, and had not anticipated any further trouble. We had on a terrific load of eggs, as it was just before Christmas. We were travelling along nicely when suddenly the engine petered out. We drew to the side of the road, wondering whatever we should do. It was just after 7 a.m., much too early for many people to be around, so we left on our winking lights, walked to the nearest farm and asked if we could phone home for help.

My son-in-law Robin came out with his huge Volvo estate car to help us get our eggs to market, but his hatchback door was frozen fast and they could not open it, so we started to pile the eggs through the driving-seat door. They then decided that one would push the door from inside and the other would pull it from the outside. With a crunching sound the door opened and we thankfully loaded up about a third of our eggs. They sat me on my assistant's knee, but I was so cramped with my head touching the roof of the car that I felt terribly claustrophobic. I cried: "Ivor let me out. I cannot ride to Loughborough like this!" So I stayed in the van until my son Michael came with his tractor and a blow-lamp. He got the van going again, but after one more mile it came to another full stop. This time two pipes had burst, so we were hopelessly stranded. Robin came back for another load and I went with him, leaving Michael to arrange for the van to be towed into a garage for repairs.

Everything seems to have a funny side. Ivor, my assistant, told me afterwards that, as they neared the market place with the first load, he saw many of our customers on their way home. As they were late arriving, the market place was congested with vans unloading and people shopping, which necessitated a very slow advance of our load of eggs. Ivor said it was laughable to see our customers following the car's progress, hoping to be among the first in the queue to be served. It was like the Pied Piper.

Our customers were grand that terrible morning. As soon as the eggs were out the car, they were sold. The queue became longer and longer until nearly dinner time, when at long last we were able to have a coffee and set the stall out in its usual immaculate order. That morning we were told repeatedly that we deserved a medal, not letting our customers down during such wicked weather. Although all

138

the stalls were erected, many stall holders had been unable to get through. It was so cold that an egg that got broken was frosted hard within minutes, and all our eggs had to be covered down to protect them from frost.

The van cost over £30 to repair. Then, coming home the following week, the diesel froze once again. But Sidney, my eldest son, managed to start his petrol-engined Japanese pick-up and towed the van home. The trouble then was how in the wide world could the van be towed into the garage. I suggested that, if I drove it, the men could push it, but the snow was so hard packed they could not get a foothold, so Sidney pushed it in with his pick-up, placing a plank on the back bumper, with two men holding it in place while I steered the van forward. I breathed a sigh of relief as we all partook of a drink of warming neat whiskey.

10

Eggstraordinary

SERVING on our market stall brought me many friends. I loved going, and I could tell many stories, both happy and sad, of the happenings around that stall. A few old-age pensioners would sometimes ask if I would sell then just one egg. "Of course I will, my dear," I said, and then I would pop a couple of slightly cracked eggs in the box alongside their one egg. The next week, seeing their faces when they thanked me was a sight for sore eyes. I had one sweet old lady whom I learned to love. She bought three eggs each week until one week she said: "I want six large eggs this week, Mrs Smith." I realized something exciting had happened for her to want six eggs, so I picked six lovely large deep brown eggs. As she tried to put them in her basket she dropped them. I shall never forget the look of horror on her face when she saw her broken eggs all over the road. I quietly filled another box and gave them to her. She took them but she just could not speak. Then she walked away. Other customers were upset, too, at seeing her distress, and they cleaned up the mess in front of my stall. The thought went through my head: "No one in this country should be so poor that breaking six eggs should be a catastrophe." The next week the lady had her usual three large eggs, but when she paid me she squeezed my hand and she whispered: "Thank you, dear, for you know what."

Another heart-warming incident was when an old lady, who also had three eggs each week, looked at me and said: "I love coming to your stall, Mrs Smith." I said: "Do you, dear? Why?" "Well!" she said, "I only have three eggs each week, and you smile at me as though I had bought three dozen." She also said that, living on her own with only an old-age pension, she could not afford to buy more, and sometimes she hardly dared to ask in shops for such small quantities of this and that because of the black looks she received.

One learned very quickly to distinguish these poor proud old ladies, who I was sure deserved a better fate, so I started saving a few cracked eggs to supplement their hard rationing. One Saturday before Christmas one of these old dears gave me a bar of chocolate. A lump so big came into my throat that I just could not speak. To think of her wanting to give me something moved me to tears. She who had so little wanted to give as well as receive.

One day a child about four years old, whose impish face only just reached the table top, looked up at me and said: "I wuv eggs, I do, I es em for my tea!" What a lovely television commercial that would have made. Much, much better than "Go smash an egg."

A lady who was a good and regular customer sent her husband one week to buy her eggs. The next week she complained bitterly that all her eggs were bad, and she had put them all down the toilet. I completely refuted this accusation. I also told her that it was not possible to find one bad egg on my stall, as they were gathered twice daily, and were only a few days old. This upset her, because she realised I did not believe her. The following week she apologized profusely. When she had told her husband what I had said, he had answered: "Oh, but I didn't get them from a lady. I got them from a man who sold sausages as well."

A more amusing incident occurred when a lady came up to the stall, saying: "Have you noticed, Mrs Smith, I have not had any eggs for the last few weeks?" When I said: "No, sorry, I hadn't noticed." She went on to inform me that she had boiled an egg for tea, and had found a fully-formed chicken in it. That experience had completely turned her against eggs for a long while. I answered: "You may have boiled an egg with a chicken in it, but you certainly didn't buy it from my stall. That is an absolute impossibility, as my eggs are gathered twice a day and I have not got a cockerel on the place." She furiously asked: "What difference does that make?" When I told her that an egg had to be fertilized before a chicken could form, she still maintained she had never bought eggs from anyone but me. A few hours later she returned, saying she had thought a lot about what I had said. She had suddenly realized that her daughter had borrowed a half-dozen eggs, later returning another half-dozen she had bought from a farm. "That is the answer to that," she said.

Only once did I have a real complaint that proved true. Three customers on the same day said their eggs tasted funny. The first said he had bought eggs from us for years and never had they ever tasted anything but fresh, but this lot had been awful. He could see I did not believe him, and he walked away, never to come to my stall again. The second complaint was made by a young housewife who said even her dog would not eat them. This second complaint by a well-liked regular customer bothered me greatly, so I told her that hers was the second complaint that day and I gave her a replacement dozen eggs. When a third lady said some of her eggs tasted funny, I was really alarmed. I asked: "What did they taste like?" She answered: "As though they had been in disinfectant." My helper and I noticed that each complaint was about the medium-sized eggs, and when disinfectant was mentioned the penny dropped. These eggs had been put against a window, which had been smashed when our food lorry had backed into it. A new window frame had been fitted and painted with creosote. The eggs, being porous, had become contaminated — just the top trays that reached up near the window. How thankful I was we had discovered the cause, and could make things right with our valued customers.

One morning one of our farmhouse-door customers said: "I have a very unusual complaint, Mrs Smith, about the eggs I bought last week." He went on to explain that a number of them were hard-boiled on one side only, the other side being exactly as it should be. I thought at first he was joking. I laughed and said: "That is a sheer impossibility." "No," he said, "I am quite serious. Those eggs were definitely hard boiled on one side only. I do not want a refund because all the eggs were perfectly fresh, but it was so funny to crack an egg into the pan and find this very puzzling sight." After he had gone, I gave a lot of thought to trying to solve this mystery. I stood in the back-kitchen looking at the stack of eggs ready for sale, when I noticed Sid had put them on a stand near my electric cooker and where we boiled our electric kettle. Then the penny dropped. I remembered that the previous week Sid had boiled the kettle nearly dry, and the spout must have been steaming away right into the side of the stack of eggs, cooking them on one side only. Thank goodness, another problem was solved. I moved the eggs to a safer place and gave my family strict instructions never to place another stack of eggs in that place.

One could go on and on about the experiences we have had on our market stalls. One day a young woman came panting up to the stall, declaring she had just bought two dozen eggs and had left them on our stall. We knew full well we had never seen this lady, let alone served her with two dozen eggs. One would always remember a new customer who had bought that number. I told her that if she left any eggs on our stall, they would have been put on one side and marked "left", with how much had been paid. She stormed and abused us, but in the end had to concede she had not bought any eggs.

I was telling some of these stories to my sister Edna, and she quoted a saying I had never heard before: "Give some people the world, and they would push you off the edge of it." I realized, while keeping an egg-stall, how easy it would be to make a lot of money by dishonesty. For example, a very old lady with bad eyesight gave me two brand-new five-pound notes which were stuck together. When I gave one back to her, she said: "Oh dear! I thought I had given you a one pound note. You see my sight is so bad, but thank you very much." Another time an old lady left her handbag, which was very old and tattered. As we were so busy, we put it on one side, and forgot all about it until late afternoon. We then decided to look into the bag to see if we could discover an address. We were shaken at what we found: a huge bundle of five-pound notes. There must have been upwards of £300. We were in a dilemma. I thought we should take it to the police station as soon as the market closed, but then on an envelope we saw a phone number which my assistant rang three times without any result. Just before we closed up in readiness for home, I saw this old lady walking around in a dazed sort of way. I called to her, and asked her if she was alright. She said: "I have lost my handbag, and my husband is wild with me." I asked her: "What does your handbag look like?" She gave an exact description of the bag left on our stall. When I handed it over to her, she just looked stunned and walked away. But she came back the next Saturday, and thanked us for saving her bag, and asked how much she owed us. I replied: "Nothing, my dear, I am almost as pleased to give you back your bag as you are to receive it."

One could hardly believe the kind of things left on our stall. During one day we were left: a pair of corsets, the owner of which we traced by the name of the maker, as they were specially made for this lady; a brand-new suit, which had the tailor's name on the box; two lengths of material which a lady claimed later that day; and one pound of cooked ham with a couple of pounds of brussel sprouts. These last were not claimed, so we ate the ham over the weekend, but the following Saturday a lady asked: "Did I leave some ham and sprouts on your stall last Saturday?" I answered: "Yes, how much did it cost you, because we ate it and will pay you for it."

I had one very confused old lady who, when we changed over to decimal currency, could not work it out at all. She used to bring a five-pound note in an envelope wrapped in tissue paper, and placed underneath everything else in her basket. She turned her back to the other customers while she searched for this package, then handed it to me, whispering: "Please change it for me. You are the only one I can trust." I felt happy to think she trusted me, but felt sad that she had no near friend to help her.

Another tiny, shy-looking old dear bought half a dozen eggs, and when my assistant gave her the change for her one-pound note, she looked so frightened and upset, saying: "I gave you a five-pound note." My assistant said: "No, my dear, you gave me a one-pound note." But she insisted tearfully: "I did! I did give you a five-pound note." He appealed to me as to what he should do and, looking at her distressed face, I said: "Give her the change for five pounds." When she had gone, he said: "Mrs Smith, she definitely only gave me a one-pound note." So we decided to watch out for this innocent-looking old lady in case she tried this on again. Sure enough, a few months afterwards she came once more to our stall. She tried it, but she knew by our faces we had rumbled her and she walked away.

Every afternoon a dust-cart comes round the market, clearing away all the rubbish. We always put ours in a blue plastic bag. One afternoon my assistant threw in another plastic bag, thinking it just an extra bag of rubbish. "Oh dear!" I said as I watched the van chewing all my week's groceries into its innards, along with a pork pie.

We have an old man customer who is very deaf and swears in nearly every sentence he speaks. I got a bit tired of this kind of talk, week after week, especially because, like most deaf people, he shouted all the time. Other nearby stall-holders used to wait to hear this old man shouting at me, so one Saturday, after he had been more abrasive than ever, I looked straight at him and shouted, oh so loudly, to make sure he heard what I was saying, that I had served him week after week, politely, and with a smile, and that if ever he swore at me once more, I should refuse to serve him. He walked away without saying another word. Along with our neighbouring stall-holders we were eager to see if he would come again, and if so, how he would react to my telling him off. He came back and, to our great surprise, his first words were: "One dozen eggs, please, me duck," and when I had served him: "Thank you very much, me duck." Since then, all those years ago, he only swore once, so I reminded him once again: "No swearing at my stall."

I think the worst of all our market

stall difficulties is torrential rain with the strong winds blowing down the market place. Everything gets saturated. I remember once, when my granddaughter Gaynor was helping me, we were both wet through to our skin. Gaynor phoned home asking that we be brought a change of clothing, even shoes. They did not bring any underclothing, so we changed in turn behind the stall as best we could and left our damp underwear on. I thought we both would get bad colds, but neither of us was any the worse for the wetting.

I remember one day when Sid was ill and I was left to manage the stall on my own. The wind was so bad on the journey down, it seemed to sway the van, which had on quite a heavy load. I thought to myself: "I do hope our stall is still standing." Fortunately it was, but many of them lay all over the road and footpaths. Some stall-holders had to take their wares home again, as those stalls in direct line of the wind just would not stay up. The wind was so bad that day I just could not fix the back cloth. I was giving up in despair when a man on one of the fish-stalls kindly offered to help me. We struggled together but could not fix it. The wind fetched it out of our hands every time we thought we were going to make it. My good friend shouted: "Missus, ain't it a bugger!" I did not say it, but I did think it was.

In spite of all these difficulties, I love being at my market stall, where I have made so many friends. Sometimes one feels very sad when a very old customer does not turn up for her eggs, and then, perhaps a few weeks later, a friend will come to tell me she has passed away. Then again, one will notice a customer going downhill so rapidly that you know that very soon she will be unable to come. I think that the best thing having a market stall has taught me is the natural honesty of ninety-eight per cent of my customers. If I make a mistake either way, they tell me. That is as it should be, and that is how I like it. Generally, we do not hear about the goodies, only the baddies.

When my first book "Memories of a Country Girlhood" was published, I was given permission to sell it on my egg-stall. I was amazed and thrilled at the number of my customers who wanted to read my simple stories, stories that I had been telling my own children, and then my grandchildren, for years. My delight knew no bounds when they told me how much they had enjoyed reading it. I had had two thousand printed, with part of a legacy left to me by my brother John Wootton, who had died of leukemia. Twenty pence of each book my friends and I sold were donated to leukemia research. Shops in Loughborough and the surrounding districts sold hundreds of copies. In under six months around 1500 books had been sold, during which time I lived in a state of happy shock at such a large number being sold.

11

Family Developments

WHEN I was around fifty years old, I seemed to lose some of my usual energy and to be always feeling tired. This was so unlike me, but I thought: "Well, I'm fifty years old. I cannot expect to feel thirty all my life." Yet in my heart I knew something was really wrong. Then I started to feel intermittent tummy pains. Then came the day when I cooked a lovely evening meal: steak and kidney pie, with a dropped batter for afters. Everyone was replete, but there was one small bit of pudding left. I asked everyone if they could eat that tiny left-over piece, but all said they were too full already. I laughed and made a remark I had so often heard Sid's mother say: "Better bust your belly than waste good grub." And that was just what I did. Apparently my tummy pains and tired feeling were caused by an appendicitis. That same night the pain came on again, worse than ever. I was so restless I even kept Sid awake. By morning I was extremely ill. Sid phoned our Doctor Brown, who immediately sent me into hospital, saying as he left: "And don't take a bath before you go." But I did. I dared not go into hospital without having a bath. How silly one can be, going against doctors orders. Perhaps that warm bath hastened the abscess to perforate. I was operated on during that afternoon, but I never realized until many days afterwards that I had been in danger of losing my life. Thank God for that wonderful penicillin which saved me.

I shall always remember coming out of the anaesthetic. The wireless was playing a lovely haunting kind of tune I had never heard before. I could not make out if it was a song or a hymn. When I was completely with it again, I mentioned this beautiful music to the girl in the next bed. She said: "I cannot remember what was on just at that time, but could you sing it for me?" I could not remember it all because I was coming and going, but

I managed enough for her to recognize that moving Christmas song by Harry Bellafonte, "Mary's Boy Child". When I got home I bought the record, playing it continually until I knew it off by heart. When our young vicar came to see me, I told him about it, and asked him if I could sing this most lovely thing in church at our Christmas service. I wanted to sing this song as a thanksgiving to God, that my life had been saved to come home to my family again, and to the joy of all those lovely precious things, which cost nothing, like walking in the sunshine and rain, seeing and smelling the countryside, and being able to gaze at the beautiful sunsets we see in England. I sang most of the contralto solos in our church, but never did I feel so much gratitude as I did while singing Mary's Boy Child. I was told afterwards that many of the congregation had tears in their eyes because they knew that I had sung that carol or song just to say simply "Thank you, God."

A few years later, when our son David had finished his year in France, he did a teacher's training diploma at King's

College, London, then obtained teaching jobs in Surrey grammar schools, first in Surbiton, then in Wallington, where he stayed for three years. He then gave us the bombshell news that he had accepted a position in Newfoundland as an assistant professor of French at Memorial University, St. John's, starting in September 1960 at a salary of $6000. I saw him off at Loughborough station, watching him wave until the train disappeared from sight. I felt bereft of the son who had always been so thoughtful and helpful throughout his life in our family. As I drove home, the feeling came over me like a cloud that this parting would be for a long, long time. I garaged the car, and walked into our farmhouse, trying hard to meet my family with a cheerful smile. I just could not manage it. I burst into uncontrollable weeping, racing into the sitting-room to cry out my misery. Then one day I saw my little daughter Lizbeth peering at me through the window, looking so upset and miserable, and all because of my incomprehensible behaviour. I said to myself: "For goodness' sake, woman, pull yourself together! You're making everyone around you miserable. How do you think other women coped during the war, when their sons were away for years fighting for our country?" After this I calmed down, and brought my mind to the stark fact that David had made his own choice of emigrating and that I had just got to accustom myself to this and get on with my life without him, even though in my heart, and by what Sid always called my uncanny intuition, I felt this emigrating would turn out to be for my lifetime at least.

This proved too true. David met a Norwegian girl named Olaug Synnevåg, fell in love with her, became engaged, and after a while he brought her over to England. I well remember David introducing me as they got out of the car. Olaug was so shy, and in a most beautiful voice, with a very attractive accent, she held my hand saying: "Do you mind David marrying a foreign girl?" I loved her on sight, and unhesitatingly answered: "Not at all, but do come in." I had run outside to meet them half way, and there we stood in the farmyard

159

during this conversation. Olaug stayed with us for a week, then they travelled to Norway where they were married.

Sid was not well at this time. He had suffered a bad fall on the farm, damaging a kidney, and afterwards he became a diabetic. As we had just managed to get him stabilized, he did not want to risk hotel food. We offered to pay Sidney and Mary's expenses to go to the wedding. They jumped at this offer and we enjoyed having their three children. We were happy to feel that David had some of his own family at his wedding.

We so enjoyed having Olaug to stay with us. There was no language difficulty, as Olaug spoke perfect English, although sometimes a puzzled look would come over her face, as on the occasion when she offered to wash up, and I asked her if she would like to borrow a pinny. She could not think what a pinny was. They came over to England about every other year, staying three or four weeks. They now have two daughters, the first named Ingrid, the second named Catherine. In 1963 David obtained a job in Toronto, where they bought a house and settled down to Canadian life. After a few years David bought a bigger house in a lovely part of Toronto where they still reside.

My mother was now eighty-six years old and, although in reasonably good health, was very deaf and nearly blind with cataracts on both eyes. She would not consider an operation, so we had to read to her. This was a great trouble to her, as through all her life she was an avid reader. I have seen her many times reading a book while breast-feeding her babies. Dad used to tell her she read far too much, but this was her greatest recreation, and could be indulged while in her own home. Mother rarely spent a holiday away from home, but she loved the game of whist, attending most of the whist drives held in our village. All my mother's life she had rather a large goitre in her neck. She had been told this could kill her, and she should have an operation to remove it, which of course she refused to do. In the end, when she was eighty-six, the goitre collapsed on to the vein leading to the heart, causing an abnormally slow heartbeat. A specialist, who came to examine her, said he could operate, but there was only a twenty per cent chance of recovery. Mother refused the operation saying: "Please let me die in my own bed." Mother lived a few weeks with this slow heartbeat, then passed away. Oh! how her family missed her, especially for her wise counsel, when we were in any way troubled. No one ever had a better mother. Although she loved each one of us, she definitely did not spoil us. She was kind, but firm, and we children knew better than to do things that were really bad, although we got into mischievous pranks quite often.

How time passes! Our sons Sidney and David had families of their own, and our third son Michael was head over heels in love with a girl named Helen Gamble, who lived in a village around seven miles away called Seagrave. The twins were in their teens. Lizbeth was apprenticed to a hairdresser and Richard was at Downing College, Cambridge, studying for a metallurgy degree. Sid and I were now a middle-aged couple, but oh! how happy we had been working together and bringing up our family. Like other people we had suffered our bad times, illnesses and the loss of loved ones, the occasional bad harvest, and animals dying, causing severe monetary losses, but we shared everything together: joy at the good things given to us, and a deep close sympathy when one of us was deeply troubled.

Our greatest joy had been watching our five children growing up into good citizens, sharing and listening to their ambitions, then trying to help them realize their dreams. Both Sid and I strongly believed that children should be encouraged to do the things in life they wanted to do, as a square peg in a round hole was to be avoided. I remember only once when we disagreed on something that really mattered, and that was when David won a county major scholarship to Leeds University. Sid wanted him to stay with us working on the farm, but I knew that David, although an excellent worker on the farm, longed for the academic life of college and then teaching. At the early age of two and a half years David loved books, spending hours on the rug, lying on his tummy, hands under his chin, looking at his elder brother Sidney's picture encyclopedia. His Grandma Smith nicknamed him "the Professor" even at that age. I also knew of the anxiety he tried to hide, in case his father insisted on his making farming his career. I always thought that in his heart Sid realized the truth of the matter, and after long and serious consultations together, he was persuaded to consent to David taking up the major scholarship he had worked so hard to obtain. How right that decision proved to be. David gained his B.A. degree, afterwards his doctorate, and actually became a professor. But the thing that pleased me most was to see his absolute happiness in gaining the life work of his dreams.

On the day his degree was presented, Sid and I travelled up to Leeds to be there. We made an early start, so that David could show us round the university before we went to his lodgings for a midday meal. His landlady cooked a marvellous lunch. One of David's friends who lived there whispered to me: "Mrs Smith, do not think this kind of dinner is usual. It certainly isn't." I did not let on that we had provided the huge cockerel as our share towards the dinner. Everyone was so replete, all we wanted was to sit and let our dinner go down, but we had to be away almost immediately. The hall was crammed full of people which made it extremely warm.

Now, although we were exceedingly proud to be there on such an occasion to see David in his robes, the ceremony was very boring. The same words were said by the vice-chancellor to each and every student gaining degrees. A very stout lady on my left fell asleep, snoring gently, and giving an occasional jump. Poor Sid tried so hard to keep awake, but what with the warm room and that huge meal, he too fell fast asleep. I did not know whether to laugh or to feel embarrassed when he suddenly woke up, saying in a loud voice, before he realized where he was: "I dreamt I was cleaning a pond out." I shushed him with a hard nudge, before he could say any more, but quite half the people in the room must have heard what he said. Most of them were highly amused, judging by the laughter that seemed to me a long time before it died down, even waking up the fat lady on my left.

Michael became engaged to Helen, and they were married at the little church at Seagrave. Helen looked lovely, wearing a white dress with a train. Lizbeth, Helen's friend Wendy Reed, and a friend's little girl were her bridesmaids, wearing blue dresses, and her nephew acted as page. One could not help but notice that the little page-boy was walking lame, seeming to be in considerable pain all through the service, and during all the time the photos were taken. His mother was quite cross with him, saying: "What is the matter, child?" "My shoe hurts," he cried. "It hurts ever so badly." His mother told him that size shoe could not possibly hurt him, but the poor little lad cried harder than ever, so his mother took off the offending shoe and found a hard ball of screwed-up tissue paper pushed into the toe of the shoe. Poor little lad! The wedding reception was held at a nearby hotel called Rothley Court, surrounded by beautiful gardens and lawns. They spent their honeymoon in Penzance.

To close this chapter the way it began,

I want to tell of an unusual experience in hospital. I had been taken in for a minor operation which my doctor said was necessary, otherwise I would become a semi-invalid for the rest of my life. How right he was — my health since then has been excellent.

When I was admitted into the ward, a young girl from Rempstone, a village two miles away from Wymeswold, was just coming round after an appendicitis operation. During our ten days stay, Sandra Beeby and I became good friends, and I like to think we helped each other overcome the depression and boredom of those long days in hospital.

One day Sandra was playing patience, with cards spread over the bed, when suddenly she gathered up the cards and shuffled them furiously time after time. I said to her: "What's the matter dear?" She answered: "Oh! I'm fed up with doing nothing." I said: "Cheer up, Sandra. Only a few more days and you'll be home again. But come into my bed and I'll have a game of 'Beggar my neighbour'." Before I had finished speaking, she sprang out of her bed and into mine, and there we had played for around one hour when the sister appeared in the doorway. The look of shock on her face was quite severe. She raised her arms, saying: "Well, I never! In all my life I have never seen two in one bed in hospital." We were not reprimanded, perhaps because we were in the pay-bed ward. Years afterwards my brother John was in that same ward with the same sister who remembered the two-in-a-bed incident.

Over the years Sandra and I were always pleased to meet each other again but, sad to relate, she became very ill with cancer and died at the early age of thirty.

12

The Women's Institute

CANADA was the birth place of the Women's Institute movement of which it has been said: "The organization is one of the most peaceful and helpful factors in making possible a wholesome life, comfort, happiness and greater prosperity." It was founded by Mrs Adelaide Hoodless of Hamilton, Ontario, who had lost her eighteen-month-old son, needlessly, from drinking impure milk. She determined that she would do all in her power to help others, and to bring within reach of all women the education necessary to prevent similar tragedies. Mrs Hoodless began her campaign with Household Science classes for schools, and then conceived the idea of rural women banding together to improve physical, intellectual and cultural conditions in the home and to raise the standard of homemaking. With the help of Mr Erland Lee of the Farmers' Institute of Ontario, the first Women's Institute in the world was organized at Stoney Creek, Ontario, on February 19th, 1897, and has never ceased to function. One hundred and one women attended that first meeting, which was a tremendous number, considering how sparsely settled that area was in 1897.

What a great debt of gratitude Institute members all over the world owe to those far-sighted Canadians for the wonderful heritage they have bequeathed to all of us. We must all try to live up to our noble motto: "For Home and Country."

It was eighty-six years later, in 1983, when I was writing this book, that the Wymeswold Women's Institute celebrated its fiftieth anniversary with a party in the village hall. The lady who was instrumental in founding our institute was Mrs Bell Tawse, the wife of a surgeon who lived at Wymeswold Hall. At the first meeting she was elected president, Miss Florrie Smith, the village primary school teacher, was elected secretary, and Mrs

Garner the treasurer. Eleven members were present. At the second meeting the attendance was again eleven, and a committee of four was formed to arrange entertainment. One of the four was to manage the refreshments, for which the members were asked to pay one penny — twopence if they brought a friend.

The minutes of those early monthly meetings make it clear that the following names were the people who pioneered those difficult times of getting established: Mrs Bell Tawse, Miss Florrie Smith, Mrs Garner, Mrs Daft, Mrs Spencer, Mrs E. Mills, Mrs Hall, Miss McNair, Mrs George Smith, Mrs Warner Wootton, Miss Charles, Mrs Bartram, Miss Greasley, Mrs E. James, Miss Lottie Wooton, Miss Sue Hickling, Mrs S. Smith, Miss Jean Bell Tawse and Mrs Harry Jalland. These stalwart, courageous women arranged competitions, concerts, parties, demonstrations, outings and debates.

The debate I remember best was about summer time and was called "The Advantages of Summer Time". The trouble was nearly every member was against summer time, and no one would speak in its favour. After much discussion it was decided that the debate must take place, and several members must speak in its favour, even though it would be against their convictions. Why in the world they chose me to be their main speaker, I did not know, but I certainly found it hard going, spouting about the advantages of summer time, only to be soundly booed at my quite dramatic ending, but it was good fun, and all taken in good part.

In those early days a charge was made for the hall of five shillings in the winter, and two and six in the summer, raised later to seven and sixpence. Delegates' expenses to London amounted to nineteen shillings for fares, and ten shillings for other expenses. After a dressed doll competition, the dolls were to be sold for not more than one shilling. The mind boggles at this astounding price. I expect the dolls were bought at Woolworth's Sixpenny Store (years ago everything in Woolworth's cost no more than sixpence), then they would be dressed in odd remnants found lying around. One shilling and sixpence was charged by the W.I. for the hire of a half gross of their china.

On reading the minutes of the meetings to arrange the New Year children's parties, one could not help but notice that the orders for food were, as near as possible, equally divided between the Wymeswold shopkeepers. They ran something like this: buns, ten dozen, Skinner's; plain cakes, Bartram's; four loaves, Walker's; nuts, Brown's; other things, Taylor's. During the war, evacuees were invited to the children's parties, bringing the number up to one hundred and twenty. Food was scarce, and a special permit was received for tea, sugar, margarine and milk. Most other foods were begged from Institute members. Entertainment was provided by Mr Tebbit, a conjurer from Loughborough. At one party the R.A.F. gave a concert which was followed by games and dancing.

Wymeswold Women's Institute has had many exceptional presidents, starting with Mrs Bell Tawse. In later years we were extremely proud that our president (and my daughter-in-law), Mrs Mary Smith, was elected County Chairman. That honour has since been bestowed on Mrs June Taylor of Loughborough, who had earlier been an active member of the Wymeswold Women's Institute and had served as secretary for part of that time. Over the years we have had many able secretaries and treasurers, along with delegates and other officers. For example, Mrs Arthur Daft was treasurer for many years. When Mrs Beall came to live in Wymeswold, she became our delegate. At all the meetings she took down all particulars in shorthand, then read them to our members straight from the shorthand notes. We must also be grateful to the late Mrs Gladys Spencer, and Mrs May Mills for their great contribution on the musical and entertainment side of our W.I. activities. In later years a choir was formed which was called the Gladys Spencer Choir. The late Mrs Jane Mills will never be forgotten by any person who heard her sing: her beautiful voice held her audience enthralled. Wymeswold Women's Institute members were lucky to have her as one of them, and were very proud of her success in gaining awards for her solos. We also remember with love Mrs Barbara Birkle for her dedicated work within our W.I. Sadly we lost her in the prime of life.

Another outstanding personality is our own Joan Duce who, in spite of her disability caused by arthritis, takes an active part in entertaining our members. She has written many plays, and produces them to the delight of many people. Joan has also composed a number of poems, which have charmed W.I. members. Her plays and poems have won many awards. Wymeswold W.I. has been lucky in having a number of members with outstanding ability who have won many awards for various crafts, produce and flower arranging. One notable trophy, won twice, was the Triple Crown Trophy, at Brooksby, for most points gained over three years. Other members have been successful in quiz shows and the ladies' skittle team has done well, too.

Here are some of the other activities of the W.I. Members who owned cars and undertook the job of driving for Meals on Wheels. They were allocated sixpence per mile petrol allowance. During 1965 members made a scrapbook of notable happenings in the village during that year. Great interest has since been shown in the book. Carol singing was first started by members who pulled a milk trolley to carry the tiny organ and the organist, Mrs Barbara Birkle. In later years a tractor and trailer were lent by Mr Tony Birkle. One can imagine the fun they had singing carols while riding in a farm trailer. Over the years many hundreds of pounds have been raised by W.I. members singing carols round the village in aid of cancer research.

Outings of various kinds have been enjoyed: visiting theatres, agricultural shows, concerts, seaside places and different factories. The educational visit I remember best was to Bourneville chocolate factory. It was a fascinating experience watching the making of chocolate from beginning to end.

I thought I would find the research and writing about the W.I. hard going, but with the willing help of Susan Jalland, Bunty Herrick, Margaret Norris, Shirley

Barrett, Iris Tyler and Mrs Jean Hodson, daughter of our founder Mrs Bell Tawse, I have thoroughly enjoyed it, and I thank all those who have helped in composing this chapter.

13

The Church

THE Church of England residents in our village were looking forward to a new vicar, a young man from Leicester, the Reverend Laurence Jackson. Mr Jackson will be remembered for the terrific effort he made to restore our village church of St. Mary's. During the war little had been done for our church, only necessary repairs. Mr Jackson encouraged all the village residents to work to obtain money to pay for this huge restoration. First the roof was put in order, to stop all the damp coming through, which had made sad work of the inside plaster. When all the new plastering was done, our beautiful church received several coats of white paint. Then the ladies formed a band of cleaners, who scrubbed and polished for many weeks. Another set of ladies formed a sewing club and

did beautiful work on the fabric of the church. They worked for several years on one outstanding project — kneelers for the choir-stalls. They also made long kneelers for the chancel rails where communion was taken. Susan Jalland, my friend and workmate, made brown denim jeans which were sold and made a lot of money towards the restoration. A lady named Mrs Huston gave a beautiful new altar which was in natural oak. A few years afterwards a lady named Mrs Richardson gave a carpet which was laid the length of the middle aisle and up the chancel to the altar steps. Everyone was delighted at the beautiful restoration of our church which is regarded as one of the largest and most beautiful village churches in all England. We have Mr Jackson to thank for organizing all our efforts.

I had taken little part in all this work as Mr Jackson had asked me, being a dressmaker, to make new cassocks and surplices for the choir. New ones were badly needed as the old ones were in ribbons. I said I would make as many as I could, but asked where I was to obtain the money to buy the many yards of material. Mr Jackson grinned and said: "We shall have to work for it." We decided to hold a weekly dance, our record player providing the music. I made enquiries about buying the materials wholesale, and found I could buy rolls of white cambric of good quality for two shillings and sixpence a yard. As soon as our weekly dances had gained enough money to buy one roll, I set about cutting some of the oldest of the surplices up as patterns for the different sizes. I made around twenty-four surplices in different sizes to fit boys and girls of ten years old up to men who were six feet tall with a forty-inch chest. I worked every moment I could, sometimes until midnight. By the time the surplices were finished we had enough money to buy black material for the first four cassocks. They proved much harder work for me, as my eyes were beginning to feel the strain, and going from dazzling white to black was a big contrast. When I had finished about six cassocks, I started one for Sid, but had to give up after that, because I could not see to do the buttonholes, and had to have them done by a machine at a Singer sewing-machine shop. Sid refused to allow me to work on any more black material. I was so sorry not to be able to make the complete set of cassocks. The vicar said I had done more than my share, and was not to damage my eyes by making any more.

While Mr Jackson was our vicar, he organized a Youth Fellowship for all denominations. After the first youth leader retired, he asked if Sid and I would take it on. This we did with the help of Mr Michael Burton who was legless. He was marvellous in every way. With the help of the teenage boys he fitted the loudspeakers, bringing them from his home in his invalid three-wheeler motor-car. The way he climbed the ten steps into the village hall was incredibly clever. There was one thing Michael Burton said to me that I shall always remember. We had just finished dancing a quickstep to a very lively tune, when I asked him: "What dance are you having next, Michael?" He looked at me and said: "Mrs Smith, can we have this one again?" I think he saw my look of puzzlement, as the children had clapped it so long and we had already had several encores. Then he said: "It is such a fast tune and I am so fascinated watching your feet." Without answering Michael, I turned to Sid and started this quickstep again for him alone. I was crying all through the dance; thinking what a great man he was, sitting there enjoying the movement of our feet, when he had no feet of his own and would have given all he had to be able to dance again. This amazing man and his wife adopted two little girls. I always thought what lucky children they were to have such wonderful parents. When Michael left the village, our youth fellowship was never quite the same again.

Another moving incident occurred when Sid and I were dancing the Gay Gordons and my eyes caught the look of enjoyment on the face of a friend whose husband had brought her in a wheelchair. She had been crippled with arthritis for many years, but it brought a lump into my throat to realize she could not walk and yet she enjoyed watching us dance. Life can be so unfair.

One year we were hosts to a number of members from the surrounding youth fellowships, some from many miles away. Our members' parents were asked if they would accommodate one or more of these youngsters for one night. They responded so generously that only three were left, so I took these three home, where they stayed until well into the following day.

That youth fellowship gathering was the best we ever had, so good that the one the following week seemed so flat I was glad to go home. We realized after this special meeting that a feeling of dissatisfaction was creeping into our youth fellowship. We always had a half-hour discussion at the beginning of the meeting, where the members could state any grievance, or suggest anything new that could be introduced for the benefit of the club. The dissastifaction I had sensed soon came out. A boy around fifteen wanted to spend all the evening dancing Rock and Roll. Many hands were raised in favour of this, others looked dubious. I thought the best plan was to talk to them in the following way. I explained that if they Rocked and Rolled all night, they would not learn anything else, and in a few years, when Rock and Roll went out of fashion and they went to real dances, they would find themselves sit-outs, because they had never learned ballroom dancing. I told them they would hate it if they liked a certain person and wanted to ask for a dance, but had not the courage to ask because of their inability to dance themselves. I also told them they would not need Sid and myself to teach them Rock and Roll, so we could retire from the youth leadership. After this talk, it was put to the vote, with an overwhelming number voting to carry on as usual. One boy stood up and said: "Your raight, Mrs Smith. I wor at a dance at Loughborough, and longed to ask a gel for a dance, but I daren't cos I couldn't do it. Please Mrs Smith, will you teach me the veleta?" That evening I taught this boy the veleta. Oh my poor toes, they were so badly hurt, but it was worth it to get the fellowship back on an even keel again.

We always had our ups and downs. One evening, just before the end, four strange boys walked into the room and sat down. Sid and I looked at each other, wondering what to do about these very rough-looking characters. We smelled trouble, but did not want to cause trouble ourselves by turning them out, and we hoped they would behave themselves. They sat quietly and we began to feel a little happier when suddenly one of our boys raced into the kitchen for a glass of water, then raced outside with it. I noticed that three of the strangers had gone, so I ran outside to see just what was amiss. One of our boys had been attacked and knocked unconscious. Apparently the strangers thought he had taken one of their girl friends out from a dance at their village the previous night, but it was not that boy at all. I told them: "I think you have killed him. We must fetch the police." With that they cleared off, and we got the boy into the hall where he came round.

Over the next few weeks, we began to realize there was friction in our youth fellowship club, headed by a sixteen-year-old girl. This girl was smashing looking with a terrific personality. She seemed to have the power to influence many of the others in discontent. We tried our very best without any result until one evening one of the girls brought in a Charleston record, saying: "I know you can't teach us the Charleston, Mrs Smith, but may we listen to the record?" "Of course you may," I answered. "Give it to Mr Burton and he will play it for you." Now this Charleston dance was very popular when I was a teenager and, without boasting, I was quite good at it. Throughout my married life, whenever a Charleston tune was played on the wireless or television, I loved to get up and lose myself in this crazy dance. So without saying a word, as soon as Michael put it on the record player, I gaily danced the Charleston, winding my way to the middle of the room, when I happened to see this girl, who seemed dissatisfied with our work, staring at me with an incredulous look on her face. "Ah!" I wondered. "Is this how I am going to get through to her?" It sure was, as the next morning on the school bus she said to my daughter Lizbeth: "Oh, Liz, can't your mother do the Charleston fine! Do you think she would teach us how to do it?" I told Lizbeth to tell her that, if she liked, she could choose six boys and six girls and bring them to our home and I would teach them the Charleston in our huge living-kitchen.

We moved the table outside and placed the chairs around the walls. I made one condition: they must promise me that at the next youth fellowship meeting each one of them would teach one other, as I had taught them. This they faithfully did, and within one month we managed to have all the youth fellowship members dancing the Charleston, some of course much better than others. I was delighted to find all dissatisfaction disappeared after this party-dance was learned, and that this girl did everything she could to help me in my work for the youth of our village. I was so pleased, as I hated divisions in our youth club.

Then something happened that made me realize Sid and I were really appreciated by our young members. It was when I was rushed to hospital with a perforated appendix. I was extremely ill, but injections of penicillin saved my life.

It was a number of weeks before I could return to the youth fellowship. When I did, I was overcome by the wonderful reception I was given. They clapped and clapped, shouting their welcome. There was even a huge iced cake, besides normal refreshments.

This wonderful welcome back did much to help me on the odd occasion when I was feeling that perhaps someone younger than I could do the job better. I was then in my fifties. Sid and I carried on for many years, until Sid became ill with a dreadful bout of sciatica which kept him in bed for three months. I had always realized that Sid's quiet influence had a great deal to do with keeping good order among our young people, so greatly did they respect him. I tried hard to manage without him, but the rougher element of our members got harder and harder to control, and in the end I resigned my work as youth leader. I was very unhappy to give up, as I loved working for the benefit of our young people, but without Sid to help keep order and partner me in teaching them to dance, I seemed unable to carry on. Perhaps the real reason was that Sid was so ill and in such terrible pain, necessitating morphine injections, that I hated leaving him in someone else's care even for those few hours a week.

Our vicar, the Reverend Bennett, was terribly upset. He begged me to reconsider, but I really could not. I was feeling very tired with constant nursing and really bad nights with little sleep. Then there was Sid's work with the poultry I had to share with Michael. Fortunately I had wonderful friends during that bad time, to two of whom I shall be eternally grateful. Kath, Sid's sister, came nearly every day, and when Sid was well enough they played the game of Lexicon, having a one shilling bet on each game, which caused a lot of fun. After the whole afternoon's play they would finish about even. Then there was Mr Turner who came to watch the horse-racing on television, and who put bets on for Sid. It really was a pleasure watching the horses, hoping their choice would win. Sid did quite a lot of betting on both horses and dogs, and his gambles were often very successful. I did not agree with so much gambling, but was pleased to know something gave him pleasure during this awful time of being bed-ridden.

By this time Michael and Helen were married and we were seriously contemplating semi-retirement. Michael and Helen shared our farm-house, using that part of the house that years ago had been made self-contained by my brother Bill and his wife Phyllis. Helen was a great help to me, especially on Saturdays when I was at my market-stall all day. She cooked and looked after my family, besides the nursing of Sid.

We decided to build a bungalow in the field where our poultry farm was situated. Planning permission was obtained, then my brothers started the building. We had been told that Sid would always have to be careful in the jobs he undertook, but he would have hated to live an entirely idle life, so we thought semi-retirement with several thousand head of poultry would be ideal for us. My health was good, and I could help a great deal, living in a new bungalow with the poultry houses in the same field. We prepared for the move, leaving Michael and Helen as tenants in the farm where Sid and I had spent so many hard-working happy years, first as tenants, and later as owners of Wysall Lane End Farm, and where we had raised our family of five children. After so many happy years of working and building up the farm, there was a certain amount of sadness at the final leaving, which was certainly lightened by the fact that we were leaving another generation of Smiths to carry on the farm we both loved so much. Our family in the new bungalow would be reduced to ourselves and our teenage twins. Richard was in his last year at Downing College, Cambridge, and Lizbeth was working in Loughborough as an assistant hairdresser.

We moved into our new home on April 1st, 1966, where we hoped for many years of happy semi-retirement. This did not materialize, for nine weeks after moving in I lost my beloved Sid, with a massive thrombosis. His death shattered our lives.

Writing this trilogy about my life, in which Sid played so great a part, I have lived again the pleasure and pain of the past. These books have helped me considerably and added a new dimension to my life. The many letters of appreciation I have received have encouraged me to continue writing. Therefore, hopefully, my fourth book will be published in due time, relating our life without Sid, my several visits to Canada to see David and his family, one special month in Kenya with Richard and his family, and above all the joy of seeing my fourteen grandchildren and one great-granddaughter growing up.

NEVER TOO LATE

To my fourteen grandchildren
and to Eleanor,
my one great-grandchild

Foreword

The success of my trilogy about country folk — '"Memories of a Country Girlhood', 'Seven Pennies in My Hand' and 'Many Fingers in the Pie' — has greatly encouraged me to continue writing. Many people have said to me: "Please do not stop writing. We enjoy your stories so much." As I myself have enjoyed writing them, I shall endeavour to relate how I had to rebuild my life without the love and support of my husband who died after a heart attack at the age of 61 years. I shall also tell how my children and I built up our flock of poultry from a few thousand birds to 8,200.

Two of my spare-time activities — foreign travel and writing — show that it is never too late to start. Since I lost Sid I have travelled entirely on my own several times to Canada, spent one month in Kenya, and enjoyed several other holidays abroad. One of my life-long wishes has been gratified — a mini-cruise on a great liner, in my case the beautiful Q.E.2. To think I reached the age of seventy before these things happened.

It was also in my seventies that I started writing, which led to my addressing meetings about my books. During this period I have enjoyed a happy relationship with my children and grandchildren, and now have one great-grandchild. For these reasons I have chosen 'Never Too Late' as the title of this fourth book.

Again I would like to thank the many people who have written me letters of appreciation which I am sorry I am not always able to answer, and for all the phone calls and visits my readers have made. I want you to know I am grateful for every one of them.

Finally, I would like to thank Marilyn Palmer for typing the manuscript, as well as my granddaughter Gaynor for designing the cover, and my friend Susan Jalland for doing the illustrations, and my son David for editing the text.

Wymeswold, 14 November 1986

14

Semi-retirement

APRIL 1st 1960 was the day my husband Sid and I retired from our 124-acre farm at Wysall Lane End, Wymeswold. There we had worked hard, but happily, for over thirty years, bringing up our family of five children, three of whom were by this time married. John Sidney, our first-born, had married a beautiful dark-haired girl from Chester named Mary Brennand. They had three children: Kevin, Marcus and Gaynor. Sidney had been extremely lucky in renting from Trinity College, Cambridge, a farm which he later bought when the college sold its Wymeswold estate. Our second son, David Warner, had married a Norwegian girl, Olaug Synnevåg, whom he had met while working as a French professor at Memorial University in St. John's, Newfoundland. They had two daughters, Ingrid and Catherine, and had settled in Toronto, Canada. Our third son, Michael William, had married a pretty girl named Helen Gamble, who lived in the village of Seagrave around seven miles from Wymeswold. They had two children, Brian and Julia. It was Michael who took over the tenancy of our farm as the fourth generation of the Smith family to farm it. Our fourth son, Richard Gordon, was still at Downing College, Cambridge, and his twin sister, Elizabeth Helen, was an apprentice in the hairdressing business.

With the 19-year-old twins we moved into a new bungalow, which we had built in one of the farm fields, where we had earlier started a new poultry venture — we kept laying hens in a controlled environment and sold the eggs on a market-stall in the nearby town of Loughborough. The bungalow was built facing south with our dining-kitchen and living room on the front. The three bedrooms and bathroom were at the back, overlooking our poultry houses and the space that was to become our orchard and kitchen-garden. The house was centrally heated with all mod. cons. The door of our kitchen and the back-door of our

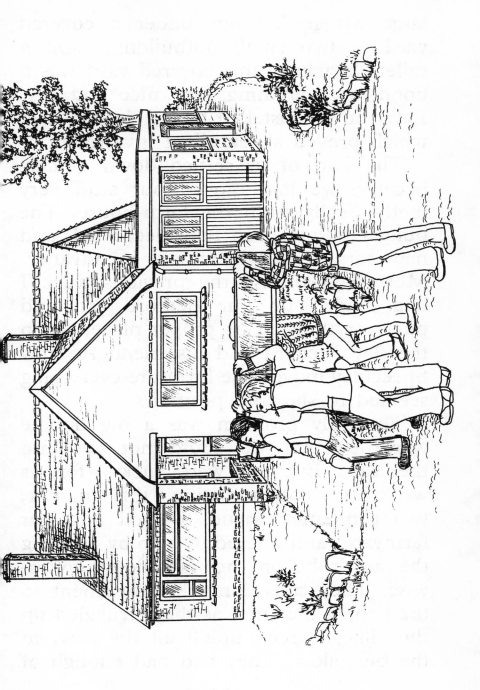

large garage led out under a covered yard to two small outbuildings and a toilet. In winter this covered yard was a boon, as everything kept nice and dry. Later on we installed here a deep-freezer which proved an excellent investment.

The four of us settled down quickly because we had moved our stuff very methodically from the farm-house. The bungalow had been fully decorated, and new carpets had been laid in advance. Most days during the previous week I had loaded up our Bedford van and put everything in its proper place, so on the day Richard and his friend Andrew Speechley moved the furniture everything seemed to slip into position.

The only problem was a big double wardrobe that we could not get into the van. But we were lucky, for as we were contemplating this matter, two gentlemen friends walked into our farmyard, and offered to help by carrying the wardrobe on their shoulders coffin-wise. They caused much amusement to the people they met as they struggled up the village street, uphill all the way, to the bungalow. They had had enough of this cumbersome weighty wardrobe by the time they installed it in our bedroom.

Another amusing incident on that last day of moving occurred after we had finished tea and were having a well-earned rest watching television in our new home. Sid, who had been suffering a bad bout of sciatica and had not been allowed to help move anything, suddenly disappeared. We thought he was taking a look round outside, deciding what needed to be done to make the surrounding grassland into some sort of garden. But no, he had unloaded the last of the stuff out of the van and spread it all over the garage floor, filling every available space with Wellington boots, shoes, pots and pans, and last-minute articles which I had meticulously loaded to enable me at my leisure to find their rightful place in our new home. I was aghast to see them mixed up all over the floor around the van. Sid was quite upset when he saw my displeasure. He said he thought he was helping to unload this last lot, bless him. I then had to search for everything out of this litter, bending my weary back to pick things off the floor instead of at a nice easy height off the van.

Friends of ours, Mr. Daft and his daughter Beryl, started building a bungalow at the same time as we started ours, and there was great speculation as to who would be settled first. They beat us by around three weeks. When Beryl came to see us a few days after we moved in, she exclaimed: "Why! You are quite straight. I'm not yet." When I returned the visit, I could see just what she meant. But there, all my life order has been a fetish with me — I just cannot work with disorder around me.

Our work on the poultry farm was much easier because we lived in the same field as the poultry-house and did not have to walk up from the home farm, where we had left Michael and his wife Helen. Our life at our new home was supposed to be a kind of semi-retirement. We had just a three-acre field, and around 3,500 hens kept in battery-houses, and we raised chicks to replace the older hens when these had to go.

I always hated to see our old hens go

204

away in a huge lorry, as I knew they were going to be killed for food, but in farming that is something one has to learn to live with. But I feel so happy on the day Michael brings up our lovely new replacement pullets: it is a fine sight for a poultry farmer to see a spotless poultry-house full of these beautifully feathered birds.

Sid and I looked forward to a happy semi-retirement as neither of us could ever lead an idle life. Unfortunately, Sid was still not allowed to work because of a dreadful bout of sciatica from which he was still suffering. This meant I had to work as hard as ever, but I loved it. I was finding the housework so very easy in our new bungalow that I had plenty of energy for gathering and grading eggs for our market-stall in Loughborough. This work was not hard, but time-consuming. The hard work, like lifting half-hundred weight bags of meal for feeding the hens, was done by Michael who came every morning for this job.

The cleaning-out was done each day by electricity, taking about half an hour. This sounds quite an easy job, but one had to stick by certain rules while the electric motors were taking out the manure. One day, much to my regret, I did not stick to the rule: I put my arm across the conveyor-wire and got caught in the cogs by my coat-sleeve. Fortunately I was in a position where I could just reach the switch with my finger-tip. Only in the nick of time did I manage to turn it off. Even then I was stuck fast with my elbow in the works. My thoughts were chaotic. What could I do? I knew it might be hours before anyone came. My arm was hurting like mad, even worse when I tried to pull it out. After a while I thought that if I could tear my coat sleeve out bit by bit, I might lessen the tight grip it had on my elbow. This was a long, weary and painful job, but in the end it worked, and after several agonizing pulls my arm was free, but the rest of my sleeve was still stuck in the cog wheel. I was then able to reach the main switch, reverse the machinery and release the sleeve. I was trembling all over, thinking that one second longer and my elbow would have been crushed to bits, and that I had been lucky to get away with an arm that was just black and blue for several weeks. All this trauma for one careless moment, but it taught me a lesson I never forgot.

When Sid felt well enough, we started to plan out our garden. We decided that, owing to the steep rise of the ground in front of our bungalow, we would obtain stone to build low walls to prevent the soil from spilling out on to the drive. We had been so lucky in making our drive, as several months before the bungalow was built, a gentleman whom we did not know called at our farm and asked Sid if he would take on the job of moving a lot of waste material from old buildings he was having demolished. He said he would pay well for this work, as the rubble needed moving away immediately the buildings were down, since there was no room on the property to store it. He thought this stuff would be used for the farm gateways. I know many men would have taken advantage of this lucrative offer, but my Sid, being so straight, told him of our great need for hardcore as a foundation for our new drive. This business had come at a very opportune time, so he offered to cart the material away without charge for the mutual benefit of both parties.

Our men started to dig out the soil with one tractor, while another took it to fill in the uneven ground which was to be lawns and gardens. Not a barrow-load of soil was wasted. Another tractor and trailer started bringing in the hardcore. In a matter of days three parts of our hundred-yard drive had been completed with this free material. The next thing was to ring the Shepshed quarry for the gravel to finish off the job. We were thrilled with our three-parts-finished drive which was now halted by lack of hardcore, but we were kept busy with the laying-out of the gardens.

Advice on this matter poured in from our friends, but ever since the foundations of the bungalow had been dug, I had spent much of my spare time thinking and planning just how we would like it. We planted a large bed of that pink beautiful Queen Elizabeth rose, and a smaller one of a rose called Peace. On a forty-yard border we had red and cream roses in alternate beds. On the raised beds in front of the bungalow we set red roses surrounded by cream ones in front of the kitchen window, and pink ones surrounded by red in front of the sitting-room window. Between each rose tree I planted a King Alfred daffodil bulb.

We then set about obtaining stone for the walls and for edging these beds and borders. We managed to buy most of this from a friend, Mr. Vic Collington, who was a road building contractor and had heaps and heaps of just the kind of stone we needed. When we had used all he had, we thought we would have to buy the rest from the Mountsorrel quarry, so one day I drove to Mountsorrel, where I asked a lady the way to the quarry. Much to my surprise, she asked me what I wanted to go there for. When I answered: "To buy stone to build some walls around my garden", she said: "I live just here and in our yard we have lots of stone I would be glad to be rid of." She got into the car and took me home and there showed me the stone, which was just the kind we needed. When I offered to pay for the stone, she said: "No, no, this rubbish is so unsightly and it has been here so long, and I want to get rid of it so I can make a garden." I was absolutely delighted with this lovely stone and again I insisted I pay for it. But no, she would not hear of it, so when Michael and his workmate, David Sheppard, took the tractor and trailer to bring home the stone, I sent the lady several trays of new-laid eggs.

David, Richard and his friend, Andrew Speechley, did most of the building work. The walls looked really beautiful and had cost so little. Richard also built a three-foot stone wall around a culvert where rain water from several dykes converged. He built an archway which has stood the test of time, adding to the beauty of the surroundings.

When we had built the small stone walls, I sowed some aubrietia seed which grew in and around the walls. In spring the garden looks delightful with the daffodils such a bright yellow and the aubrietia many shades of purple and mauve. Then in June the roses start to bloom right on until September.

Sadly my beloved Sid did not live to see the first roses start to bloom.

15

The Loss of Sid

WE had hoped Sid would soon be allowed to help with the work on our poultry-farm. He was still a very strong man. Lifting bags of meal was child's play to him if only this dreadful sciatica would leave him. He hated this idle life, as he called it. After several weeks he was at last able to play his beloved game of bowls again. Our lives started to settle down and we lived through a short period of very great happiness. I felt how lucky we were, until suddenly, out of the blue, our wonderful life was shattered: my beloved Sid suffered a heart attack while playing bowls on the Loughborough Beacon Road green. He was brought home and put to bed, and I anxiously awaited the doctor's verdict. He told me this was a warning attack: Sid's heart had not suffered real damage, he would have to stay in bed a few days, and he would have to take care the rest of his life.

Although I could not talk about it, my life became blighted with the secret dread that he would suffer another attack. I watched him furtively most of the time. Every morning when I woke up, I put out my hand over to his bed to feel if he was alright. (We had been reluctantly forced into using single beds because of the pain any movement of mine caused him to suffer, while the sciatica was so bad. I have always been a restless creature in bed.) I hoped and prayed that I was hiding my anxiety from both Sid and my family.

After a few days Sid was up and about again. During the time of his convalescence we were both invited to the wedding of Janet Sheppard, the daughter of my cousin Ron and Lizbeth's best friend. With Sid still feeling a bit under the weather, we were unable to accept their kind invitation. Much to our delight and surprise, Janet and her brand-new husband left the wedding festivities and came to our house carrying a plate each of the same kind of luscious food as they and their guests had enjoyed. Sid was very moved at the lovely sight of Janet in her white wedding-gown and by her thoughtfulness on this her very special day. Janet had always been a great favourite with Sid, and I remember so well that after he had wished them much happiness, he turned to her husband and said: "Be good to her. You have a lovely girl here."

There was a special reason why Sid was so fond of Janet. When she was only a few months old, her Grandma Sheppard, who was my auntie, brought her in her pram for us to see her. Sid could not take his eyes from her. After they had left, he said to me: "Nell, isn't she lovely? I wish we could have one like her. Should we try again?" Within three months I was pregnant at the age of thirty-nine, and with twins, so Sid always thought Janet was the cause of our having the daughter we had longed for so much.

One evening Lizbeth and I sat eating nuts and raisins, when Lizbeth said: "Could Dad have some nuts and raisins, Mum?" I answered: "Nuts, not raisins", because of his diabetes. I looked up to ask Sid if he would like some nuts. Oh dear! I was shocked and alarmed by his looks, and I knew he was suffering the second heart attack I had dreaded for several weeks. We sent for the doctor and with Michael's help we put Sid to bed. Our wonderful Doctor Brown stayed with Sid for several hours. He told us Sid had only a fifty-fifty chance of recovery. Then in the early hours of the next morning Sid suffered another massive thrombosis, and he slipped, oh so peacefully and quietly, away from us. Dr. Brown had stayed with Sid right to the end. I shall always be grateful for the comfort he gave me and my family.

Our lives in just a few hours were shattered. A man so strong as Sid, one just could not believe he had gone. I kept thinking: "It was only last night when a jazzy tune on the television made Sid take me in his arms and dance me round the room." I missed and grieved for the lovely times we had danced and danced, never tiring of dancing with each other. Now I had to face with courage life without that wonderful man.

A German saying that the Rev. Lawrence Jackson once said to me helps a lot at times like this: "Money lost, little lost; health lost, much lost; courage lost, all lost." Many people asked if I felt bitter, but strangely I did not. I felt stunned but I kept thinking: "I have had more happiness during the forty odd years I have known Sid than many people ever experience at all." My beloved Sid reminded me of the old saying: "Steel true and blade straight, the great Creator made my mate."

My children were a great comfort to me. David flew home from Canada and stayed a week. Richard, who still had one exam to write in his finals at Cambridge, left and came home. I think they gave him average marks for that exam. I remember so little of what happened those first few months, but one thing I clearly remember was David putting his arm around me and saying: "You know, mother, there is still something in life for you." I could not think that at the time, but how right he was: my children, their spouses and their children have been a great comfort and joy to me over the last twenty years.

A week before Sid died, our son Michael's first baby was born down at the farm. This child, a boy they called Brian, meant a great deal to me, and I prayed he would grow up and be a man like his grandfather. He would never know, but Sid held him just once. As a toddler, he became my shadow, always happy to be with me gathering eggs, and supposedly helping in the garden, more often than not carting the soil by the small bucketful on to the drive.

He was with me one day in one of our poultry-houses when he suddenly disappeared. I found him in the egg-room by the side of a box of eggs where he was picking one egg up, holding it as high as his little arm would go, then letting it fall plonk into a bucket where he had dropped and broken around two dozen eggs. Brian at that time was three years old, and he received his first smack from me. Really it was no more than a love-tap, but the tone of my voice chastising him and my sending him into the house to Lizbeth were more than he

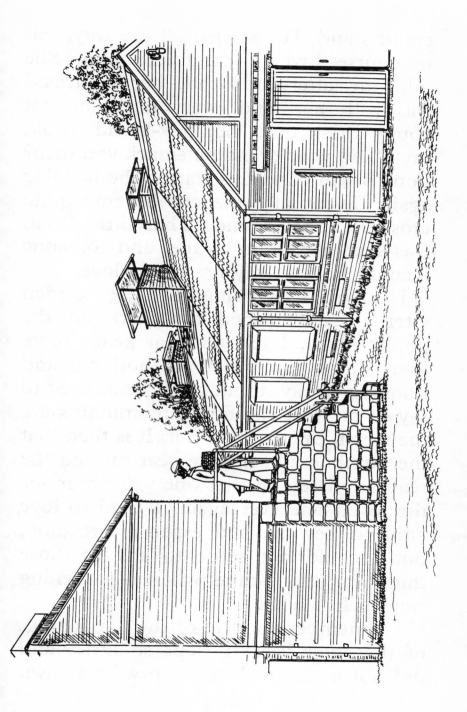

could stand. He howled all the way, but of course Lizbeth comforted him. She told me afterwards that her boyfriend was with her, and every time she got young Brian quiet her boy-friend would say: "Did your grandma smack you then? Poor Brian!" and this started the howling again. Eventually Lizbeth became quite cross with her friend. That little Brian was such a comfort to me, and someone I could hold in my arms and love.

I enjoyed working in the garden after I had finished my work on the poultry-farm. I felt more at peace there than sitting around doing nothing, and thinking, always thinking. Friends used to say to me that the first three months are the worst, but they are not. It is then that the numbness begins to wear off and the realization sets in that one will never see the loved one ever again. I used to love knitting, sewing, and especially reading, but I could not settle to any of those things for a long time, whereas gardening was such a help.

I remember so little of the happenings of that first year. I slept so little, and did not eat enough to keep a bird alive, losing three stones. My family was so concerned it was decided I should go to Canada and stay with David for a few weeks. Sid's sister Kathleen decided to come with me, so we booked our flight and made the necessary arrangements.

Kathleen's sixteen-year-old son Robert took my place on the poultry-farm, thoroughly enjoying the responsibility of looking after so many hens. He had one dramatic happening, the story of which he told with relish. We had recently had a new poultry-house built, the kind called Californian. This house is built over a six-foot pit. One end, where two tons of poultry meal were stored, should have been reinforced with strong beams, but the builders had omitted them. One morning Robert opened the door to find that the floor had collapsed and the better part of two tons of meal had fallen into the pit below.

Robert could not enter to feed the birds with no floor to walk on, so he rushed back into the house, searched for and found the number of the Nottingham builders who had built the house only a matter of months before, and told them, not asked them, to come immediately, as the poultry-house floor they had built had collapsed. Their answer was: "We cannot come today. We are much too busy." But Robert would not take no for an answer. He told them they were responsible for the disaster, and if they did not turn up that day, he would hold them responsible for the loss of egg production and wasted food. He also told them it was a matter of life or death to those birds nearest the collapsed floor, as the cages were hanging in mid-air. The builders came and were very glad they did, as those birds were in great danger. Many sixteen-year-old boys might have panicked, but not young Robert.

Lizbeth, too, was wonderful: keeping house, cooking, cleaning and helping with the poultry. These two youngsters were very proud to be trusted with the complete management of 3,500 laying hens. Michael looked after the baby chicks and was always around to be called if needed.

They also had a good time entertaining their friends in the evening. In fact, it was while Kathleen and I were in Canada that

Lizbeth met her future husband, Robin Lilwall, who at that time worked for a food firm called Levers. He had come to our place to try to obtain an order for poultry meal, and from that time no other boy seemed to interest Lizbeth.

After her father died Lizbeth gave up her hairdressing job in Loughborough to help me on the farm. She did all the housework and cooking, and looked after several hundred birds that her father had given her.

16

First Trip to Canada

KATHLEEN and I looked forward to our trip to Canada with great excitement. I had never been on a plane before, but I was not the slightest bit afraid. We travelled down to Gatwick, staying overnight in a hotel in the old part of Crawley, five or six miles from the airport. We were awakened by the management at six o'clock, had breakfast, and then a taxi called to take us to the airport. We had a marvellous flight with Caledonian to Kennedy Airport, then took an onward flight to Toronto, where we were met by David. There Kathleen and I spent a nice quiet week, then David took us to America to visit Kathleen's step-daughter, Diana, who lived at Rolling Meadows, several miles on the other side of Chicago.

I was so impressed by the roads as we drove through Chicago: sometimes we looked down on the town, at other times we looked up. When the roads were built, they had blasted through the hills, and built bridges over the valleys. In some parts the road had six lanes on each side, and we travelled through the town at seventy miles an hour. When our M.1 was built, we thought it was amazing to have three lanes each side. Once one of my Canadian grandchildren asked me: "Grandma, why are your roads so narrow in England?" I could only answer by saying: "Because our country is so small in comparison to Canada, we cannot spare the room." The wide, wonderful roads of America and Canada must be the envy of every British visitor to those countries.

David and I stayed with Diana for one night, then we travelled home by way of Detroit, the city whose centre was burned out in the riots of 1967. David drove through the middle of the city so we could see the Renaissance Centre's splendid new buildings which had been recently erected. We called to see a friend of David's who had a blind young wife. In spite of this handicap she had prepared a perfect meal which we thoroughly enjoyed, after which we were on our way again to Toronto. I believe we travelled about six hundred miles each way, but people living in those countries think nothing of travelling a hundred miles just to see a play.

During my stay in Toronto David was determined I should have a game of bowls, so he took me to a green at the bottom of their road, where a huge banner across the pavilion read: "All Visitors Welcome". David asked if there was a chance of a game for his mother, but they just did not want to know us. At the second green the result was the same. Then David said: "We will try one other green." But he did not think we would have any luck, as this third green was very special and was used for international bowling.

I smiled at David, and asked him to leave the talking to me this time. At the other greens I had received the impression they thought I was an inexperienced bowler, a visitor who just wanted a game to pass the time. I put on my blazer which had my Leicestershire Ladies

County Bowling Association badge on the pocket. I approached a lady and asked her if they could fit me in for a game. I added that I had skipped for my county of Leicestershire in England, and would be able to take my place reasonably well. This lady seemed interested in somebody from England wanting a game in Canada. She introduced me to the president who gave me a delightful welcome and immediately fitted me into a game.

The following day the club was having a special tournament which they called The Queen Elizabeth Cup after the previous queen, now the Queen Mother. They played triples with both ladies and men. I played second with a gentleman skip and lead. We played all day and into the night on a floodlit green. Luckily I played one of my best ever games, and our rink reached the finals but we did not win it.

I played with a ladies' team the following day. When I was introduced to the other ladies as Ellen, one of them said: "Last night I was sick and tired to death of hearing that name. My husband played in the tournament yesterday with a lady named Ellen, and I had to sit and listen to him singing her praises all the blessed night." I chuckled when I told her I was that Ellen. She got her own back when she was able to tell her husband that her side had beaten my side, and that I had played nothing out of the ordinary. I had not either, but that is the game of bowls. I expect that after playing late the night before, I was a bit tired. I was very proud, though, to have been allowed to play on that beautiful green with such a grand lot of people.

My holiday in Canada was nearly over, so I wanted to spend those last few days at home with my family.

The arrangements for my return were that David was to take me by car to New York, where we would stay a couple of nights, meeting Kathleen at La Guardia Airport where she was to fly in from Chicago. We stayed at the La Guardia Hotel but Kathleen was nervous at being put in a room by herself a long way from us, so we decided to ask the management if the three of us could share one room. David had said to me: "Mother, straighten your shoulders, and I will walk with a stoop and we will sign in as Mr. and Mrs. Smith." (This was quite true of course. In fact, David, who had recently grown a beard, had once been mistakenly taken for my husband which had not pleased him at all.) We told the receptionist of Kathleen's fear and asked if it would be possible for her to share a room with us. She said she would ask the manager. When she came back, she said they could arrange a room that would be quite satisfactory. The room had one double bed with a large bookcase along one side, mostly filled with books and plants, which made the single bed the other side completely private. Needless to say, David used the single bed, and we took turns in the small bathroom to change into our night clothes.

How right Kathleen was to feel happier with us. The next morning, as we looked out of our window, we saw a number of policemen and a large black van. A few moments later a body was brought out and was put in this van. We heard later that a murder had been committed.

We enjoyed our stay in New York, but I was disappointed in the lack of cleanliness in parts of this magnificent city. The streets were dirty and littered with every kind of rubbish. When I mentioned this to an American lady, she said: "Oh, yes, but did you not know there is a garbagemen's strike on at the moment?" I answered: "Really! They must have been on strike a long time, as outside the confines of the La Guardia Hotel there is a dirty old double-bed mattress with a hole in the middle that has grass growing through it." Glass jars, bottles, old tins, and old newspapers lay there. In Central Park one had to spread a newspaper on the seats before one dared sit down. I even saw several mounds of human excreta lying behind my seat, where I was watching a baseball match with black and white teenagers. Yet the outskirts of the city were beautifully kept, the grass verges were finely cut, and old men with spears were picking up the few odd bits of paper.

We enjoyed going up to the top of the Empire State Building, which I understand is the highest building in the world. We gazed at the city of New

York from such a tremendous height that the streets looked like ribbons, and the cars like match-boxes.

We visited the huge building of the United Nations, where I thought of the millions it had cost, and the billions it would cost over the years ahead for its upkeep. I hoped and prayed that through the United Nations we would secure peace, then all that cost would be worthwhile, but I wondered whether the U.N. would ever have that power.

We also went on a cruise on the River Hudson, where one could see the Manhattan skyline with all those high buildings, a sight I have never forgotten. When the boat passed the Statue of Liberty, one just could not believe it was so big.

I felt New York was an unfriendly city. The people did not care one jot for the visitors. During the afternoon David and I parted for a while, and of course, as usual since I became older, I lost my bearings. I asked three different people the way, but all I got was a shrug, and each walked away without saying a word. I knew I had not walked very far, and eventually I found my way back.

At one point I stood outside a restaurant where I watched two ladies sitting at a table in the window-recess eating their meal of one whole small chicken. They held it in their hands and ate every morsel of meat from the bones, never using a knife, and only using a fork to pick up their vegetables.

On a later occasion David went into this place to use the toilet. He seemed to me rather a long time gone. When he came out, he was grinning and said: "That pee cost me 4/6." Apparently there was an attendant there who handed him a clean towel, and then brought a clothes-brush and cleared every speck of dust from his suit. I remember the remark I made: "Well David, if a wee is going to cost me 4/6, I will keep it until we get back to the hotel." In those days we were only allowed to take a certain amount of money out of the country, so one could not possibly afford 4/6 for just that.

I certainly would not like to live in New York. The heat was terrific. When we went into the air-conditioned shops, we needed to put on our cardigans, but when we came out again, we met a blast of heat like opening a huge oven-door.

We travelled back to our hotel by the underground, where in every carriage, at each end, stood a policeman fully armed with guns and ammunition in wide leather belts. While walking through Times Square at midnight, one never met one policeman alone on a corner, but three, all thoroughly armed.

The following morning David took us to Kennedy Airport where we said goodbye to North America.

17

Richard's Marriage

AFTER arriving home, I started eating a little better, but still slept badly. Dr. Brown advised sleeping tablets, but after two nights of those I flushed them down the toilet, because they made me feel so ill. One day Lizbeth came home after visiting an auntie of Robin's who had also lost her husband. She had advised Lizbeth to buy me a bottle of sherry: I was to take it to bed with me and drink a glass of it in bed. Now I had never enjoyed wine or spirits, but anything was worth trying if it could only stop those sleepless nights, when quite often I heard the birds' morning chorus before I slept at all. I started with half a glass, and a book to read. The two together helped enormously and I started a better rhythm of sleep, sometimes gaining up to five hours, which were very welcome.

I was washing up one day when an egg customer tapped on the window. When I opened it he said: "Look what I have just found." He held out a ring with a huge diamond set in platinum. He said that, as he walked up the drive past a large heap of gravel, he had noticed something shining. On investigation he had found this beautiful ring. He wondered if any of my people had lost it. I was quite sure they had not. The gentleman left the ring with me, saying: "Perhaps you will make enquiries." I placed the ring in a drawer and forgot all about it, the state of my mind was so bad at that time. A week went by before my daughter-in-law Mary was chatting to me on the phone, when she suddenly asked if I had heard that a gentleman who travelled round the village selling very good-class carpets was advertising for a valuable ring his wife had lost in Wymeswold. It was insured for £600. "Oh, my goodness!" I cried, "I have it, I'm sure." I was so worried, I had visions of being in court for stealing by finding. I rang the village policeman and confessed to my having had the ring for a whole week. I explained how I had come by it, put it away and forgot it. The policeman said: "Don't worry about it, Mrs. Smith. I will come and fetch it immediately and see that it is returned to the owners." He then gave me their address and I wrote to them expressing my regret at forgetting about the ring, and for the anxious time I had so needlessly caused them. The carpet-man was extremely kind: he answered my letter by return post, including a £10 note to be divided between the gentleman who found it and myself. He wrote: "Please don't worry any more, Mrs. Smith. My wife is so happy to recover her ring which has great sentimental value." The next Friday my egg customer asked for news of the ring, as he had seen the advert. He was delighted with the £5, saying his daughter would now get a new dress for a wedding she was attending.

Around this time I set on a young man to help on the poultry-farm. When he said he had been away at school, I naturally thought he had been at boarding school, but it turned out to be a reform school. Oh dear! In a matter of three days he had taken out my nearly new Bedford van, and crashed it into a lorry, making the van a write-off. I had given him permission to drive it on our very long drive, but not to go on to the road, because he had no licence. I never got a penny insurance, and for a period of time I thought I might be in danger of being held responsible for the damage to the lorry. I forgave the lad, hoping he would turn over a new leaf, but he got itchy feet and moved away from the district. I bought a second-hand van for £275, which gave good service for many years, until I sold it for £150. I then bought a brand-new Commer van with a diesel engine which was in use until just recently.

I have had the help of many youngsters over the years as a poultry farmer, and in my experience they have been honest, pleasant, industrious and altogether reliable. This speaks well for the youth of today. We do not hear much about the good kids, but the baddies get all the news. We have been extremely lucky with our five children, who have been a pleasure to bring up and have always been kind and caring.

Lizbeth, who was still working with me on the farm, thought she would try to obtain a stall on Nottingham market. At that time this was not difficult, as the old market was about to be closed. However, a huge new shopping precinct, called the Victoria Centre, was already under construction, which was to include a new market, a huge car park, some flats and a new city bus station. Lizbeth's idea eventually proved an excellent one, though for close to two years she had few customers. Those who had stalls in the old market were given high priority for a place in the new complex, but in the meantime many stall-holders in the old market fell by the wayside, since their trade became worse when the buses were the first to be moved to their new quarters. Lizbeth courageously stuck it out, sometimes standing all day and only selling around fifty dozen eggs. But when the new Victoria Precinct was opened, she had a lovely little stall, where her new-laid eggs became so popular she needed to employ an assistant. Then she started to sell dairy products, specializing

236

in Stilton cheese made a few miles from our own village of Wymeswold. In due course a second stall was obtained, selling the same kind of produce, but when a very large stall became vacant in one of the best positions in the market, she sold this second one and became established with the new one. Lizbeth now employs a number of assistants.

Richard finished his education at Downing College, Cambridge, gaining his B.Sc. degree in metallurgy at the age of twenty years. During his last year at college he met the girl he eventually married. She was a nurse at Addenbrooks hospital and her name was Eirene Johnson. She had suffered the loss of both parents, and had one brother. A chance meeting changed her life: she first saw Richard when she went along with another nurse to visit his room-mate, who had spent some time in Addenbrooks hospital suffering from a severe bout of asthma. They became friends and very soon sweethearts. He brought her home several times during his last year at college, after which he obtained a job as assistant personnel officer in a steel works near Bristol.

This parting and the distance between Cambridge and Bristol could not be tolerated, so Eirene got a job in Bristol. A few days after Eirene's twenty-first birthday, they were married in our village church of St. Mary's, where Sid and I had married around forty years earlier. As Eirene had no parents to provide a wedding for her, it gave me great pleasure to see they had a day to remember. I knew that Sid would have wanted this, too. Eirene's Auntie Dorrie gave her the wedding-dress, which was white, full-length and made of satin and lace. She looked out of this world and really lovely. She had three bridesmaids: her friend Vonny, our Lizbeth and Gaynor. They were dressed in deep wine-coloured velvet dresses, and instead of flowers they carried white fur muffs, which they were glad to have, as it was a bitterly cold December day. Snow lay thick on the ground, and we all drove to church through a blinding blizzard which had miraculously cleared by the time we left the church. The photos were taken outside the church and everybody looked perished. I was very moved walking without Sid into that church where for many generations Richard's ancestors had worshipped. I was so grieved that Sid was not with us to see them married and their obvious happiness.

To this day I cannot walk into that church without feeling the loss of Sid more than at any other time, because of the deep happiness going there had given us. Even as I write about it over sixteen years later, my tears are blotting out my view of the page, but I must blow my nose and wipe my eyes or my writing will suffer. Life is surely a mixture of joy and sorrow like that wedding-day of Richard and Eirene.

After the service we travelled the eight and a half miles to Kegworth where the reception was held at the Yew Tree Inn for around fifty guests. We had a marvellous meal, the main dish being turkey, since it was so near Christmas. I lent them Sid's car to take them to the Lake District where they spent their honeymoon. They managed to rent a flat in Bristol, later buying a house. When they wanted to come home, they were so short of money they hitch-hiked both ways. I used to take them to Rempstone where they could be picked up. One morning when I dropped them the rain was pouring down and I wondered how far this lorry that gave them a lift would be travelling. Perhaps they would need several more lifts before they arrived home. Perhaps they would be saturated by the time they reached Bristol. On my journey back home my thoughts toyed with the idea of giving them Sid's car, which was rarely used since he left us. If I really needed to drive anywhere, I could always use my van. On arriving home I immediately sat down and wrote to them: "Will you hitch-hike home next week-end and I will give you your dad's car." Needless to say, they turned up and were delighted to be the owners of a really good Ford Consul car.

The time came when Lizbeth took driving lessons, so I bought a brand-new Ford Escort Estate, which we both enjoyed driving for many years. In those days it cost just over £600.

18

Poultry Stories

I HAD only just bought the new car when our poultry was smitten with Newcastle disease (fowl pest). All poultry farmers dread this deadly disease and, after the first case in the country was diagnosed, every farmer watched his birds for signs of the disease.

I do not know if it is true, but it was rumoured that fowl pest was brought into our country by a young lad from Israel who had worked on a farm whose poultry had been wiped out by the disease. He came with fowl pest in his eyes to work on an English poultry farm near the east coast. From there it crept gradually towards us in the Midlands and eventually spread over most of the country.

One Sunday morning I was doing my usual examination of our birds, when I noticed that the hens in two cages in direct line of the fan bringing in fresh air were looking decidedly sorry for themselves. "Oh dear me!" I thought, "these fans bring in the fresh air, but have they also brought in the fowl pest germs?" I felt really alarmed and rang Michael to come and look at these dejected-looking birds. He thought the same as I did. By law, when fowl pest is suspected, the owner of the birds has to report the matter to the authority concerned. The vet was here in a matter of hours. He examined all the birds, saying: "What a lovely healthy lot of birds they look! But I must kill one of the dejected-looking hens and do a post-mortem." I watched with deep apprehension as he cut into the bird. And there he found the dreaded tell-tale signs of strawberry-like rashes under the skin. Yes, our birds had started with the fowl pest. A notice was put up on our farm-gate: "Keep Out. Fowl Pest," and a straw bed soaked in disinfectant was placed in the gateway.

We were certainly in deep trouble as, after paying death duties on Sid's estate and buying the new car, my bank balance was nearly nil. And what about our market-stall, if we were not producing any eggs? We would need to buy in hundreds of dozens each week. And where in this disease-stricken country would we be able to obtain them? Our living would be gone, as the government had stopped paying compensation to farmers whose birds had fowl pest. We were lucky: Lizbeth's boyfriend, Robin, had a friend who knew of a farmer living near Boston whose birds had never caught the disease. He would sell me 360 dozen eggs each week, but he would not come near my place, nor would he allow my vehicle near his farm. Robin's friend solved the problem by offering to allow the farmer to deliver them into his garage at Grantham, where I was to fetch them when the farmer had got clear away.

In a matter of days all the birds in that house either died or were slaughtered. It was a dreadful sight to see heaps and heaps of dead hens which only a few days before were beautifully feathered birds looking their best and laying at ninety per cent production. The dead birds were put into paper sacks, loaded on to a trailer, and taken to be buried in a deep limed pit which had been dug by a contractor with a special kind of digger. Before he left the farm, the tractor and all his equipment had to be thoroughly disinfected. The cost of digging each pit was ten pounds.

Exactly a week later another lot of birds, over 2,000 this time, contracted the disease, and the same procedure went on all over again. Another week later Lizbeth's 360 birds followed suit. Out of 3,500 birds only 300 sickly-looking birds were left, which were never very productive again. We moved all these into Lizbeth's house and set about cleaning and disinfecting the affected houses with a special disinfectant that killed the fowl pest virus.

We were not allowed to bring in clean stock for a matter of six weeks, as they would be likely to catch the disease. However, I had good friends who advised me that, if I could buy in vaccinated stock which had already had the disease and had quickly recovered, I would be quite safe to do so. Fortunately, I found a farmer who had the number of pullets I required. He was not only willing to sell them but was really anxious to be rid of them, as no farmer free of the trouble would consider taking them into their flock. I was worried that these pullets might not lay well, but I was assured by the vet that they would lay very well indeed, so I made a deal with the farmer to pay half the price asked and after six weeks pay the other half, if the birds proved all right. Everything did go well, and I was delighted to pay up and look pleasant, as the eggs from these birds, and the 360 dozen I fetched from Grantham saw us through those extremely difficult times.

Although my many customers were told of the fowl pest trouble, and many knew I was buying in a large percentage of our eggs, they were very loyal and still kept buying from us. After around six months, we were on an even keel again, producing all our own eggs.

One thing worth remembering is that fowl pest can be transmitted to humans. During the middle of our trouble I began to feel dreadfully ill and had to give up work with flu-like symptoms. Yes, I had

caught fowl pest and was ill for around a week. While I was feeling so ill, Richard and Eirene were expecting their first baby and Lizbeth had arranged to go to Bristol to look after them. A baby boy was born whom they named Richard but always called Ricky to distinguish him from his father. The morning Lizbeth was to go, she came into my bedroom saying: "Mum, I think I have the fowl pest in my eyes. Do you think I ought to go to Bristol?" I sleepily sat up in bed and looked at her eyes which were red and swollen, and I knew it would be very unwise for her to go. This upset every arrangement: Richard and Eirene were expecting her that day, and a friend of Lizbeth's who had offered her a lift into Bristol, was calling for her in a little over an hour. A decision was made: we thanked her friend but declined his kind offer of a lift, and a telegram was sent to Eirene with a letter to follow. Lizbeth's eyes bothered her for around ten days.

Since that loss of over £3,000 in three weeks, we have always vaccinated our birds. The time came when the government refused to allow the farmers to vaccinate, but guaranteed that, if Newcastle disease broke out again, compensation would be paid. However, at the first alarm that pigeons had a kind of fowl pest and nothing could possibly prevent them from transmitting it to our flocks, we were allowed once again to protect our birds from this horrible disease. Had an outbreak occurred during the government-enforced cessation of vaccination, it would have proved a most expensive embarrassment.

Some really strange and queer things can happen on a poultry-farm. One day I was quietly grading eggs when I heard a hen making a weird noise. It sounded as though it was trying to crow like a cockerel. I listened a while, then crept down the line of birds until I reached the bird. I examined it and found that it was, in fact, beginning to look like a cockerel: its feet had grown bigger, its neck longer and more arched, its comb had grown to an abnormal size, and the male wattles were forming. After a few weeks this hen had really changed sex and was crowing properly. I have seen this sex-change happen to hens several times during my years as a poultry farmer.

A more frequent abnormality in a hen occurs when, from the time it is one day old, it is neither one sex nor the other. I was intrigued by this phenomenon, so one day I did a post-mortem on one of these hermaphrodites. I knew just what both a hen's and a cockerel's insides should look like. There, sure enough, the bird had the male organs, but instead of small bags of white fluid they were filled with a bloody substance.

Hens also lay the occasional queer egg. Not only do they lay eggs without shells that we call softies, but several times I have collected a four-ounce egg with a skin surrounding it, then another normal egg joined to the skin of the four-ounce one, then another soft-shelled egg joined to the normal one. Once, and only once, I gathered an egg that looked exactly like a brown velvet one with a band round the middle of a natural colour. I often wish I had got that egg blown, then it would have kept a lifetime. Now and again we gather an egg which looks exactly like a single link of sausage.

On one of my visits to Canada David was determined to show me a huge poultry-farm with 60,000 laying hens. It was near Picton, a village by the side of Lake Ontario, where David had rented a cottage for a week. Although at home we had under 10,000 birds, much of our set-up was superior, both in cage-design and especially air-flow. Also our poultry-houses are built with more space per bird. Apparently the owner had bought two old three-storey factories, restored them and filled them with laying hens. He experimented with different age-groups. Downstairs he had young pullets, on the next floor he had one-year-old hens, but on the third and top floor he had three-year-old hens. He said he would never keep hens again for three years, as the packing-station refused to have the eggs, because they were much too big, and suffered too many cracks, owing to poor shell quality.

I asked him why he had so many empty cages on the second floor. He told me that batch of birds had suffered the disease called Mareks, and he had lost a big percentage of them. I told him my poultry had escaped this trouble, but sad to say, when I arrived home, one batch of my birds had contracted the disease, too. Out of 1,500 birds I lost 800 before and during their laying period. Not only did I lose the value of the birds, I had to buy in replacements. That year I lost a packet, as a result of this horrible disease. Mareks is a kind of cancer, which takes many forms, but once seen, never forgotten. Sometimes the hens just go thin and die. At other times a limb will give way: perhaps a wing or a twisted neck, but mostly a leg which cannot hold their weight, so they start to hop. I used to pick them up as soon as they started this hippety-hop style, and get Michael to put them out of their misery, for they never, never recovered.

Nowadays a day-old chick is vaccinated against it, and very little is heard of it these days. I understand it was in England, at Houghton College, that the vaccine was developed, which has made all poultry farmers very grateful to them for saving their birds from contracting this dreadful disease.

I noticed that all the birds on this farm at Picton were debeaked and no beak had grown again as my birds' do at home. As a result there was absolutely no feather-pecking. Now this feather-pecking was one of my greatest worries, both with free-rangers and those in controlled environment. When I told him we debeaked our birds at eighteen weeks old, and that quite half their beaks grew again, he smiled and said: "That is where *we* beat *you*, Mrs. Smith." You see, I had already told him the points where our management was superior to his, so he was quite pleased to tell me about the superior way they debeaked their birds. He told me he had a machine that would debeak at one day, five days, or seven days. When I asked him if it was cruel to the chicks, he said: "Good gracious me, no! It is no more than you cutting your toe nails." I obtained all the information about this wonder-machine, and when I returned home, I rang two farmer friends and we bought one between us. We have had no trouble with feather-pecking since. If only some of these animal rights people realized that debeaking birds is not cruel, when done properly, and that it saves birds when they are older from pecking each other, sometimes to death.

19

Other Animal Stories

MANY things happened on our poultry farm, that people eating their breakfast eggs would hardly believe. Michael once reared two thousand chicks from day-olds to seven weeks of age in a building that was thought to be absolutely safe from predators of any kind. How wrong we were! One night a fox worked its way in through a sliding door which even had a nine-inch nail attaching it to the main doorpost as an extra precaution. He worked the nail three-parts out which allowed him to creep through an almost impossibly narrow nick. The next morning two hundred seven-week-old pullets lay dead or dying, some with their heads bitten off, others with such terrible wounds Michael had to kill them. We had an experienced joiner to that door to make sure this could not happen again.

Something else not quite so bad, but certainly bad enough, happened to a flock of day-old chicks, something so incredible I could forgive anyone for disbelieving this story. Once again two thousand chicks were delivered into a house that was warmed to the correct temperature by propane gas heaters. There was not a speck of dust anywhere, the floor was carpeted with the usual wood shavings six inches deep, and everything seemed perfect, when suddenly Michael saw a huge doe rat, heavy with young, race down the building and through a hole in the lining of the wall. Michael tried every way he could think of to force this rat out into the open, even putting a tube to his tractor exhaust, hoping to gas it out, but to no avail. We decided we would have to risk one or two chicks, and if the gas had not worked, try again the next day. On entering the chick-house the next morning Michael saw a huge doe rat jump out from under one of the hoovers. Luckily he managed to kill it, but noticed that the wood shavings had been trampled down, making a ribbon of a road the full length of the floor to the hole where the rat had disappeared the previous night. Michael followed this trail to a place where he heard the plaintive cheeping of several chicks. He was horrified to find 104 dead chicks. This was unbelievable that one rat, heavily pregnant, could work so hard during one night and carry that number of chicks over a ninety-foot length of floor covered in wood-shavings five or six inches deep. She sure was getting her food prepared for the birth of her babies. No wonder Michael killed her so quickly, the rat must have been literally tired to death.

Vermin are a source of trouble to every poultry farmer. The meal given to hens provides easy food to both rats and mice. The next two stories happened a number of years after the rat incident, but this seems the right time to tell them. It was after Lizbeth and Robin were married that they had a brand-new poultry-house built to hold 2,300 hens. It was what is called a Californian or deep-pit house. Being short of cash, they falsely economised by not putting a concrete floor in the pit. Towards the end of the hens' lay, the house was overrun by rats which wasted a terrific amount of food by biting holes in the food bags, letting out a lot of meal as well as what they ate. We tried shutting up the cats in the house, then using poison, but all to no purpose; the rats came in ever-increasing numbers, burrowing their way under the foundations and finding refuge in the manure in the pit. When the hens were sold, we started cleaning out the pit with the tractor which had a huge scoop that could bring out a tremendous amount of manure each time. All the dogs were brought up from the farm in readiness for the slaughter of the rats. We had a young man, David Sheppard, driving the tractor. He also carried a heavy staff and, when the rats started running out, he kept stopping the tractor and jumping off to kill them. Michael stood ready holding another staff. When I tell this story of the rats to my grandchildren, I tell them we had three lines of defence in the battle with the rats. "First, the dogs killed many as they emerged. Then David and Michael killed a lot of those that escaped the dogs. The third line of defence (a pause), you will never guess, children (another pause), well, it was your grandma with the garden-hoe. I killed four." The kids loved the last bit — grandma with the garden-hoe. By the end of the day the dogs were completely exhausted. Two went home, and could not be persuaded to return, but Michael's little old Trixie, who was making her way home across the field, turned back when Michael gave her a whistle to return. Poor old Trixie never got over the hard work of that day. We only saw four rats escape, which the dogs caught the next morning, when we counted the surprising number of over 400 dead rats.

When I tell this next story to the children, I call it "the story of the drunken mice". It happened in the same house as the rat story. The floor had been concreted, which kept out the rats, but this time, towards the end of lay, we had a great infestation of mice. It seemed funny how the vermin liked this brand-new house, when the older houses were comparatively free. We bought pounds worth of poison, but the mice would not eat it, they liked the poultry food much better. We rang the pest-control officer who informed us that the infestation was very bad, and much too large to eliminate while the birds and their food were still there. He advised us to ring him after the birds had gone, and the house had been cleaned out, as the poison would not have the desired effect if the mice could get back to their burrows in the manure, where the warmth would bring them round again. He also warned us that, if any cat or dog ate any of this poison, they would come round if placed near a warm fire. He mixed this white powder with a bowl of poultry meal and then filled a number of small plastic trays with the mixture, placing them all over the nice clean house. By this time the mice were desperately hungry and were soon devouring the mixture of meal and white powder which made them drunk, then slowed their hearts until they stopped. Michael came running to the house, calling: "Mother, do come. You will never see a sight like this ever again." He was helpless with laughter. I ran out to the poultry-house where hundreds of mice were staggering all over the place.

They were running four abreast down the food troughs until they passed out.

We thought that was the end of the drunken mice story, but it had a sequel. Ivor Jalland, our poultry manager, left out a few trays of the mixture in case the odd mouse might be left. He left the door open to allow the fresh air to circulate and a robin flew in, eating some of the left-over powder, which made it as drunk as a lord. Remembering the pest-control officer's words about the warmth, he placed the robin in his inside pocket and continued his morning's work. When he went home for his dinner, he shut it in the airing-cupboard. After dinner he fetched it out, put it into the palm of his hand and it flew away perfectly.

While on the subject of mice, I remember that, in the early years of our marriage, while living in an old thatched cottage, I had carefully conserved half of our Christmas cake for my birthday on January 8th. Being very fond of Christmas cake, I opened the cupboard door, just to pinch a small slice, when I noticed a hole in one side of the cake. I immediately thought: "Hullo! Sid has beaten me to it, but he might have used a knife, not just delved in, making such a mess." I cleared up all the crumbs, eating every currant. There seemed rather a lot of them around, with no cake adhering to them. I went back into the kitchen and accused Sid of pinching the cake and leaving such a mess. "I have not touched the cake, Nell," he cried. At first I did not believe him, I thought he was teasing, but knowing him so well, I soon realized he was speaking the truth. Nobody else could have touched the cake, so when I thought of all those currants licked clean, I screamed: "Oooer! mice! and I have eaten all those crumbs and licked-clean currants." I got out the peroxide and washed out my mouth. Sid was chuckling with laughter all the time. I could have hit him. I moved the cake to another part of the house, after cutting the outside of it away. I put the left-over pieces back in the cupboard to see if it really was the mice that had pinched my cake. Sure enough, during the night every bit of cake had disappeared, but the currants were left, licked clean.

We now keep cats, which help keep the

nuisance of mice down to a minimum, but even cats bring their troubles. We started with three, calling them the three T's: Tigger, Tommy and Tilly. Tilly and Tommy contracted cat flu. Tilly died, and Tommy, the favourite, nearly died. He was brought into the house, placed in a box near the radiator that kept warm all through the night, and was covered with an old pullover. Poor Tommy! Each night I thought would be his last. His eyes were completely closed and were full of matter, so I poured castor oil into each one, which he immediately tried to rub out but fortunately rubbed further in. The oil did good work: the next morning he opened his eyes and he completely recovered from the cat flu.

They say a cat has nine lives. Tommy certainly had another narrow escape. Late one night I heard cats fighting. I hoped it was not our Tommy, but of course it was. The next morning he looked awful: his tail was bitten half way through near the body. He sulked and went missing for several days during some wet and very cold weather. We all became worried and searched everywhere we could think of.

Eventually Ivor found him. He was very far gone, as his tail wound had become septic. I took him to the vet who cleaned the wound, then sprayed it with some dark stuff. Then he gave me penicillin tablets to beat the blood poisoning. When Tommy had disappeared, I had made the remark that I would give fifty pounds to any charity to see him come home fit and well, instead of which I had a large vet's bill.

After a few weeks Tommy was his old self again, so to save him more trouble with his fighting we decided to have him neutered. I borrowed a cat-box, but he fought his way out, bursting the cardboard box, so I put him in a paper poultry-meal sack, and tied it up with string. I entered the vet's surgery, which was full of people with their various kinds of pets: huge dogs, small dogs, and many cats, some of which were in baskets and some in expensive cages. There I sat, holding a paper sack tied up with string with something squirming inside it, causing much amusement and quite a few pitying glances. I kept undoing the string just to see if Tommy was alright and to let in a little air. When the vet came in to call my name, he looked at the sack and said: "One can see you are a farmer, Mrs. Smith. No one else ever brings their cat in a paper sack." He gave such a humorous look at all those expensive cat-cages. I was glad to get out of that surgery, away from those condescending glances.

Tigger is not a good-tempered cat. In fact, sometimes he is right vicious. But Tommy has a lovely nature and loves children. Whenever any of my grandchildren come to stay, he comes and sits on the window-sill of any room the children are in.

20

Yet More Animal Stories

ANOTHER story I remember well occurred just after Lizbeth and Robin built their bungalow in the same field as mine. Funnily enough, we had just seen the Hitchcock film called "The Birds". We had a lot of crows nesting in the trees north of our poultry houses, and when they started making their nests, they began attacking the putty in the bungalow windows to help build their nests, coming in great numbers in the early hours of the morning when no one was around. This went on for several weeks, after which Lizbeth and Robin had to have their windows reputtied.

One morning I was woken up early by a strange tapping sound I could not understand, so I looked out my bedroom window. The sun was shining brightly on the shining chrome hub of my car-wheel, where a huge black crow was fighting its mirrored image in the wheel-hub. It was furious and did not stop, even when I shouted at the wretched thing. Every morning this bird came to have another fight, so I moved my car where the morning sun did not reach it and I was able to have my sleep out.

One lovely summer evening I was working in the garden, when suddenly the peace was shattered by an awful anguished screeching, caused by a blackbird caught in the mouth of our cat Tigger. I ran to try to make Tigger drop the bird, but she evaded me by hiding in a thick hedge. As the poor bird's cries became fainter and fainter until they stopped altogether, I knew Tigger had killed it. The blackbird's mate, perched on the guttering of one of our poultry-houses, was screeching his head off. Poor old father! I knew these two birds had a brood of young ones in a nest under the roof of one of our poultry-houses. When I gathered the eggs in that house, I could hear the babies being fed: they made a chirping sound when they heard their parents enter the roof. I never knew if the babies lived with just one parent to feed them, as there were several nests under that roof. In fact, they nest there every year. In all my years living in the country I had never seen a cat kill such a large bird.

Another thing that was worrying me greatly at that time was a noise under the roof of my bungalow. First I heard a scratching sound, then after a pause a gnawing sound, and lastly the unmistakable patter of little feet across the ceiling of my bedroom. "Rats!" I thought. "In my house! How in the wide world have they found their way up there?" I sent for the pest-control officer who could not find any trace of rats, but he left some poison which Michael put under the roof, where the rats could find it, that is, everyone said, if there was a rat up there. Some people said they thought it might be birds making a noise under the eaves, but no one believed me when I still said: "I am sure it is a rat, or rats. I have heard that patter of little feet too often in the roof of one of my poultry-houses not to recognize it again." These noises became much worse. Every night they kept me awake. Then they started in the daytime, when everywhere was quiet. My family and friends still kept saying I was imagining these noises, so when they started in the day-time I began to wonder myself.

One day, just after I had finished my dinner, I was having a few minutes peace and quiet when I happened to glance out of the window, and there I saw a slight movement in the guttering of the front porch. I kept perfectly still and watched. A few seconds later a little furry face with bright eyes peered over the edge of the guttering. I watched fascinated as the rat — yes, it was a rat — looked this way and that way. Then I must have made a slight movement, for it disappeared like greased lightning along the guttering, and down the drain-pipe.

I again sent for the pest-control officer who, after much searching, found that the rat had come up the sewage pipes a matter of nearly a hundred yards. It had gained entrance because a top had been left off a grating outside a cottage being modernized at the bottom of our drive. It then found its way up the drain-pipe and along the guttering, and there gnawed its way through the soffit and under the roof.

Ivor placed some wire into the top of the drain pipe, then he found the hole which the rat had made, and fixed a new strong piece of wood over it. I well remember the remark Ivor made, as he climbed down the ladder: "That's the end of the rats, so long as I have not boarded any of them inside." That night, just before bed-time, I heard once again the pattering of little feet over the sitting-room ceiling. "Goodness!" I thought, "Ivor was right: he has shut up a rat inside." After a few minutes the rat started on its night-long work gnawing its way out, nearly at the point of its entry. I was so interested listening to the rat I just could not go to bed. Although I could not see it, I could so well imagine how it was working. First, it was the continual gnawing, then one could hear it shuffling the gnawed pieces of wood away from the hole it was working on, then there would be complete silence for a few minutes, then the gnawing, shuffling and resting would resume. I listened until four o'clock the next morning, when I went to bed and left the rat still working away. By morning it had escaped and we have had no more visits from the rats, after Ivor fixed another piece of wood over the escape-hole.

Another frightening happening took place that week. Again it was a quiet summer evening, and I was gardening in the front of my house, when suddenly there was a terrific crash, followed instantly by a girl screaming. I clambered over the wall into my neighbour's garden, where the girl's horse had wandered into the garage, which had a sump covered by a door that time had rotted. The horse had stepped on to the cover which had collapsed, letting it fall into the sump which was half full of water. The horse struggled out, a bit wet, but not much the worse, save for a bleeding mouth, caused by biting its tongue in the struggle to get out. Helen, the owner, was very distraught, but calmed down after we led the horse on to the lawn, where it started grazing, proving to her that it was not seriously hurt.

Several years later, on January 21st 1984, we heard and saw on television that America was having terrible snow storms. I made the remark that my mother always used to say that we in England would have the same kind of weather a fortnight later. One of the weather-men on television mentioned this matter, saying there was no truth in it whatsoever, but oh my goodness a fortnight later we sure had it this time! Scotland was the first to be hit, then the rest of England had many inches of snow just one fortnight after America. Our poultry-farm is not well placed to combat this sort of weather, as our roadway is a very steep hill. On the Monday Ivor tried to manoeuvre the van a matter of eighty to a hundred yards so as to load it with eggs and cheese for the Nottingham market-stall. He managed about ten yards, which took ten minutes, digging a way bit by bit. Ivor asked me to drive, while he pushed, but all to no avail, so we rang Michael down at the farm to ask him if he would bring his tractor with a fork-lift loader to try and clear the roadway. Bless him, within half an hour he had made a clearway wide enough not

only for our market van, but also for the huge food-lorry that was expected with meal for our poultry.

When this kind of weather occurs, I feel sorry for the wild birds who cannot find any of their natural food, so we make this an excuse to clean out the troughs to give the old meal to the birds. Then I take out my dust-pan and clear a space about ten yards long and eighteen inches wide on the drive opposite my window where I sit writing or reading. I sprinkle several dustpans full of this old meal — which is not really old, but we tell ourselves it is so we can feed the birds with stale meal, instead of using meal straight out of the bag, which at the moment costs £185 per ton. The birds simply love this meal, and I surely love to watch them flying into this ten-yard strip in ever-increasing numbers — all kinds of birds: teeny-weeny ones, middle-sized ones, and many of the larger blackbirds. I find it fascinating the way they eat. After their first hunger is assuaged, they start to fight. There is one huge blackbird that bosses the lot of them. He sits on the heap of snow I cleared from the drive, as though to say: "I am king of the castle." Then, of course, our cat Tommy has to put his oar in. But when he springs, the birds all fly away into the nearby trees, and as soon as Tommy disappears, back they come until that strip of ground is black over once again.

21

Lizbeth's Marriage and my Departure for Kenya

IT was in 1971 that my daughter Lizbeth decided to get married. She and Robin did not want a big wedding, so they were married at the Loughborough Registry Office, with just Richard, her twin brother, and me as witnesses. A reception was given for them at my son Sidney's Clay House Farm and later in the evening all the guests attended another reception at the Priest House Hotel in Castle Donington. The honeymoon was spent in Derbyshire.

Their first home was the small flat down at the farm, where my brother Bill had made two rooms and a cellar into a self-contained flat, when he and Phyllis were married. While they were living at the farm, my Wootton brothers built them a lovely bungalow in the same field as mine.

By this time Lizbeth's market-stalls at Nottingham were selling more eggs than we were producing, so they decided to build a poultry-house to hold 2,300 hens. This extra house enabled us to be self-supporting most of the year for all our stalls.

We bought day-old chicks, around two thousand each time, reared them to twenty weeks of age, then moved them into their laying quarters. When looking at that number of fluffy baby chicks raised from day-olds in one huge building, heated with propane gas units called hoovers, one thinks back to the time when we sat a hen on thirteen or fourteen eggs, waited three weeks for them to hatch out, and then installed them with their mothers in coops out in the yard. Rain, snow, wind and blow, the poor little chicks had to withstand it all. Many did not survive, and some were lost to predators like cats, foxes, stoats, weasels and even magpies. Nowadays it is not uncommon, when buying two thousand odd chicks, with two extra given for each hundred bought, to raise more chicks than we have paid for. Why do people listen to the shouts of the animal welfare extremists who advocate going back to the old ways, not knowing the agony some of those chicks suffered in extreme weather?

Raising birds by this method, we were able to have nearly all the sizes of eggs we needed to supply all our customers. This makes a difference in keeping our customers happy, as different families need sizes to suit their needs. For instance, those with a large number of small children need the smaller eggs. Most need the large eggs, which is fine for us, as we have more large for sale than any other size.

When Lizbeth became pregnant, she reduced her working days. By this time she had a competent staff, and Robin took charge on Saturday, even though he had a responsible job the rest of the week. Lizbeth had a bad time with her first baby which was a girl she was going to call Rachel. Sadly, the baby was stillborn. The whole family was upset about this, but a little over a year later Lizbeth had a lovely baby boy whom they named John. He was such a good baby, I used to say to Lizbeth: "You don't know you have a baby." This, of course, she did not believe, at least not until she had another baby boy who really was a little tinker right from the first. They named him Richard. After a while Lizbeth started working again for two days each week, after finding a reliable woman to look after the children.

On September 24 1977 my sister-in-law Kathleen married Charles Lewitt in our village church. Her son Robert gave her away, and my daughter-in-law Mary was her maid of honour. I remember one thing said about them in one of the speeches at the reception: "These two are such extraordinary ordinary people." They have richly deserved the happiness they have enjoyed together.

In the meantime, Richard and Eirene, who now had a second child, Carolyn, had left Bristol, sold their house and bought an old-world cottage at Kegworth, where they lived for one year while Richard took a course in business management at Loughborough College. They then packed up their bags and emigrated to Kenya, where he worked as a training officer in Mumias on a sugar plantation.

After settling in Kenya, Richard and Eirene had two more children, first a girl they named Peta, and then another girl they called Madeleine. Sad to say, little Maddie died at the age of five months. This was a cot-death tragedy that caused great sorrow for a long time. Eirene was especially depressed. Although we relations in England had never seen the baby, the sadness was with us all the time. When another letter came a few months later saying that Eirene had suffered a miscarriage and was very low in spirits, I felt I had to make the journey to Kenya to see if I could help in any way. I sent a letter by return which told them I had been to the doctor to start the necessary injections which by law one has to have before entering that country. The doctor said they would take six weeks, as at my age he dared not do them in less time. I made the necessary arrangements, and on December 29th 1977 I set out on my great adventure to Kenya.

Richard and Eirene had asked me many times to visit them, but I was afraid of the 4,000-mile journey completely on my own: I would be landed in a country where I could not speak a word of the language. The other fear was that Richard would not be there to meet me, as he had a journey of between two and three hundred miles over dreadful roads before reaching Nairobi airport. These fears had been dispelled by a letter from Eirene, giving me the address and telephone number of two of her friends living in Nairobi, who would help me if an emergency arose. I left my friends the Jallands to look after the poultry farm.

My son Sidney and all his family saw me off at the Loughborough bus station, where two buses for London waited. One, they said, was a fast one, going all the way on the M.1 motorway; the second was going through many of the Leicestershire villages before joining the motorway after Northampton. I had no hesitation in choosing the slow bus, as I had several hours to wait in London before the departure of the plane from Heathrow. After we had travelled a few miles, it started to snow, and the weather became considerably worse as we advanced further south. I arrived at Victoria bus station at 5:30 p.m. I only had to carry my case across the road to British Airways where it was weighed, and I did not see it again until reaching Nairobi. I had bought wheels for my heavy case, which I thought would be helpful to me, but they proved a nuisance, as I had to carry them all the way to Nairobi. Wheels were not permitted with the luggage, in case they damaged other cases. I also obtained my boarding ticket at Victoria, but had to wait nearly an hour for their bus, which took us right to terminal 3 at Heathrow, where we boarded the plane. I spent that hour in the restaurant, where I met a lady around my own age who was travelling on the same bus and plane. We had much in common, enjoying our chat, which was mostly about our families. Together we found it quite easy going through the formalities before boarding the plane, which was one hour late starting. The captain said we would be given a round of drinks to compensate for the delay. During a most enjoyable journey we had dinner, then breakfast about an hour before landing.

When I had left Loughborough the weather had been bitterly cold, necessitating the wearing of many warm garments. These were removed one by one, so that, when arriving at Nairobi Airport, we had on only the minimum of lightweight clothing. Most people had brought hold-alls for the discarded clothing.

The first thing I noticed on leaving the plane was three little faces peering through some railings, and three little voices shouting "Grandma! Grandma!" at the top of their lungs. The joy at seeing and hearing them was indescribable. I could not go to them, as all the passengers had to board a bus which took us to the airport buildings, where we went through all the formalities before we could obtain our luggage. I just cannot describe the meeting with Richard's family, one of whom, Peta, had been born in Kenya. After I had given hugs and kisses to Richard and the children, Eirene threw her arms around me and would not let go. She kept saying: "Thank you, Mum." In those three words and in the hug she gave me she told only too clearly the sadness she had suffered those last few months in Kenya, and the joy she felt at having someone from England, who cared deeply, visiting them for one whole month. Eventually we were all under control again.

On our way to Richard's car I picked up a wallet which had the return air-ticket sticking out of it, so I took it back to one of the desks, where I hoped the owner would find it. Then we were on our way through Nairobi to the hotel Richard had booked for the night.

In the afternoon we went shop-gazing. Richard bought Eirene a pair of beautiful gold and ivory earrings. I never imagined there could be such magnificent ivory carvings, from teeny-weeny ornaments to a whole tusk costing hundreds of pounds. I looked for a doll in national costume, which a friend had asked me to buy for her daughter who was making a collection of dolls in national costume, but I could not find one.

After putting the children to bed, leaving them in the care of a resident baby-sitter, Richard took us out to dinner and for a drive around Nairobi. Afterwards we met Peter and Jill Brown, friends they had made in Kenya, who had come to Nairobi to see Jill's parents off after a lengthy stay with them. Peter worked for the same firm, Bookers, as Richard, managing the sugar factory's machinery.

I thought Nairobi a lovely city, but very different to any other I had ever seen. Begging was rampant. Some beggars also tried to sell pornographic books, pushing an open page under your nose, hoping for a sale. Some of them were really pitiful cripples of all ages. I saw one with wasted lower limbs, but with such fantastically strong arms that he could lie on his belly and literally walk on his hands, dragging his body along. I just felt compelled to give that one some money. Eirene said: "Mother, you simply cannot give to all these beggars, you won't have any money left." At that time we were allowed to take out of the country only a limited amount of money.

22

Nairobi to Mumias

WE then started on our way home to Mumias. My son Sidney, who had visited Richard's family earlier, had warned me of the bumpy roads, but oh my goodness, I never expected such a rough ride. Poor Eirene, who sat in the back of the car with the two-year-old Peta on her knee, suffered the worst. Once we went over an extra large hole, which shot Peta out of Eirene's arms and into her face, making her lips bleed. I asked Richard to drive more slowly, but he said that if he did, the bumps would be much worse. I realized after a month in Kenya that everybody drove fast on their potholed roads. Going fast, the cars skimmed over the bumps and potholes, but on approaching the Great Rift Valley, we were forced to slow down considerably, as we were climbing for mile after mile up what seemed a wall of rock. To the left of us was the spectacular sight of the Great Rift Valley, which is the biggest valley in the world. As we looked down, we could see the wrecks of many cars and huge oil-tankers that had gone over the edge and been left to rot, as the job of recovery was almost impossible. Richard made the remark: "Perhaps it is as well to leave them as a reminder of what can so easily happen if a driver loses control and goes over the edge."

Life in Kenya is very different from life in England. I will try to describe our journey from Nairobi to Mumias which was between two and three hundred miles. We met only a few cars and practically no other vehicle passed us. We saw many donkeys, heavily laden with all kinds of produce and huge sacks full of I know not what. Herds of goats were as numerous as herds of cattle. The Kenyans, who were taking cattle to market or to be slaughtered, held them with a rope tied to a hind leg. Sometimes the car ran over these ropes, but nothing seemed to happen to hurt them. Their slaughterhouses were terrible places, just a ramshackle mud building that one could smell a mile away. Tractors were seldom seen, as the ploughing was done mostly by oxen, the kind with humps on their shoulders. Sometimes they would be ploughing with as many as six oxen. I also noticed that numerous farmers would be walking along the side of the road carrying milk cans holding anything up to two gallons of milk. Apparently these farmers walked many miles to a meeting-point where they met a lorry loaded with churns. Their milk was measured and taken away to the towns.

I was astounded by the work the women did in this country. The young women can carry tremendous weights on their heads, standing up straight and looking so graceful. But the older women had backs bent by the heavy loads they had been forced to carry all their lives. It was not unusual to see the young ones with bags of meal or rice weighing twenty-eight pounds. They also carried on their heads huge baskets full of garden produce. On the way I saw two elderly women with loads of sugar cane on their bent backs which looked larger and heavier than the women themselves. Although they were walking with backs nearly double, a man with a huge stick was following behind, carrying nothing. I wondered whether, if they stopped or faltered, he would hit them with that great stick. I learned that the women did most of the work on the small farms, even carrying their babies in slings over their backs while working.

Bicycles seemed the main kind of transport for the men, but we never saw a woman riding one. We seldom saw only one man on a bike, mostly two and sometimes three. Riders would carry huge loads of produce and lengths of wood which often stuck out across the road a couple of yards. This was a dangerous practice, as cars found great difficulty in passing them on such narrow roads.

Our first stop was to see the flamingoes on Lake Nukuru. Their feathers were a lovely delicate shade of pink. Spread over miles and miles of lake, the birds were really so breathtaking a sight that even the children were silent. Many notices asking visitors to keep quiet were posted on trees. Any sudden movement frightened the birds, making them fly away in waves of shining pink. I recently read that during the last five years the flamingoes have been gradually leaving Lake Nukuru for other lakes in the Great Rift Valley. The reason is thought to be the introduction of new types of fish which bring many more visitors to the lake.

We stayed in Nukuru for coffee and sandwiches, then we were on our way again, but not before I had done a silly thing. I posted a card in a post-box, which was really one for used stamps, but fortunately some kind person reposted it, and it arrived safely in England in due course. As we progressed on our journey, I could not help but notice many dead dogs lying in the road in various stages of decomposition. Richard said that dogs killed on their roads were never removed. Even humans were left many hours until their relatives arrived to perform their traditional wailing over the body. We were to see an instance of this later on in my stay.

I was very interested in the thorn trees which seemed to grow into the exact shape of an open umbrella. The thorns were like great six-inch nails, so sharp they would pierce right through a man's foot. I noticed in a park in Nairobi that they had protected new-laid turf by placing layers of thorn-tree branches over it, thus keeping off both man and beast.

On the roadsides were many local farmers selling their fruit. We halted in readiness for buying a few plums and peaches. Almost before we stopped we were surrounded by men holding out cardboard boxes full of these fruits. Then began the traditional bargaining.

Richard: How much for a box of plums?

Kenyan: Fifteen shillings.

Richard: Much too much.

Kenyan: Twelve shillings.

Richard: Still too much.

Eventually we bought them for less than half the asking price. The man tipped them all into the car loose — no persuasion could make him part with his cardboard shoe-box. The same thing happened when we bought the peaches. This was the month of December, and there we were buying fruit in lovely hot sunshine. I was to learn later that in Kenya new potatoes grow nearly all the year round.

We stopped for tea in a very beautiful hotel called Kericho Tea Hotel, then drove on the last lap of our journey to Mumias. Suddenly we had a rainstorm, the like of which we rarely see in England. Just as suddenly it was all over. I heard later that each storm like this one added £12,000 to the sugar company's profits because it swelled the cane. I realized we were nearing Mumias by the sugar cane sticks lying on the road which had dropped off the sugar-cane lorries.

23

Life in the Compound

THE Mumias sugar factory employs many people, both black and white, and even more men work on the sugar plantations. After nearly three hundred miles of travelling we entered the grounds of the sugar company. First we passed the shacks and houses of the Kenyan workers. These houses were much superior to the shacks we had passed on our way, but they were dreadful places at the side of even our poorest dwellings. I felt quite rich when I thought of my small bungalow in our village of Wymeswold, and I asked myself: "Why, oh why do we have all the dreadful strikes, when we have so much, so very much more than the people of Kenya?" Yet on looking into the faces of these people, one got the impression they were contented and happy, in spite of the fact that the average man's wage at that time was only five shillings per day.

We then entered the managers' compound, where a guard stood at the gates. He knew Richard, so we were allowed straight through. The compound took up many acres of ground, and was surrounded by a very high safety-fence, which was patrolled every night by guards. The managers' bungalows were really lovely. Richard and Eirene's was delightful, spacious, and well furnished, standing in around one and a half acres of ground. Richard said that, when they had first come to this place, it was just a nice house in the bush, but they had put in a lot of hard work and hired a full-time gardener to cultivate the land, and in less than five years they had trees growing thirty feet high. They now gathered their own bananas, pawpaws, and pineapples, along with potatoes, cabbages, etc. When they had first gone to Mumias, only nineteen European families lived in the compound. Now there are around forty white families.

We entered the bungalow through the side-door which led into a roomy kitchen, then into a huge room measuring around twenty feet long by fifteen feet wide. The part nearest the kitchen was used for dining, the rest of the room was furnished mostly with cane furniture (armchairs and settees), with small tables standing here and there. At the end of this room was a passage with three good-sized bedrooms, nicely furnished. Opposite the bedrooms were a bath and toilet, which had an abundance of solar-heated hot water day and night. The sun was so hot that it heated the water quick enough for us to have baths one after the other during the day without any waiting. Only on one day were we without much sun, then the water was just warm. All the floors in the bungalow were made of cement polished with a meths and boot-polish mixture to give a marble finish. In that hot country, it was so cool to the feet carpets were not needed. A veranda ran down the length of the sitting-room with the same kind of floor as the rest of the house. As it was several yards wide, many couples could dance there during the parties Richard and Eirene gave.

I was introduced to their three Kenyan servants. Joseph was their house-boy,

Selifa was jack-of-all-trades, and Sapherio was their gardener. I went to bed that first night tired but full of wonder at this country of Kenya. I was awakened by Joseph the following morning with a cup of tea. Apparently he came to work at seven o'clock and his first job was to take the family a cup of tea. Then he cleaned up their huge living-room and kitchen, after which he prepared breakfast, gave the eldest two children theirs, and got them ready for school, afterwards serving breakfast to the rest of the family. At eight o'clock Selifa came to clean the bedrooms, do the washing, the amount of which is amazing, as it is not unusual to change one's clothes several times in one day. In the afternoon, she did the ironing. One day I asked the two-year old Peta: "What is Selifa doing in the kitchen?" "Oh!" she said, "Selifa is hotting the clothes", a good description of ironing from a two-year-old.

After breakfast Eirene and I went to the works' clubhouse, where there was a beautiful swimming-pool. The children's school was behind the clubhouse and during playtime they had a lovely time, swimming and diving like fishes, or playing on the various contraptions so dear to children.

The wives in the community lived an extremely lazy life: they all had their Kenyan house-boys who did all the work for a few shillings per day and thought themselves lucky to have such a good job with a European family. As the days passed, even I got used to the idle life of the white woman in the compound.

The first Saturday I was there I was invited to the works' New Year party. We all went to the boss's house for drinks and light refreshments. The dance was most enjoyable, and the eats absolutely fabulous. The band was an all black one. They played beautifully, but when I asked if we could have the Gay Gordons, I was told that these boys would not know it or any other old-time dance, so we had to be satisfied with the new craze of doing the shakes, which everyone seemed able to do. They did play a fair share of the modern waltzes, quicksteps and slow foxtrots. I danced nearly every dance. The other Europeans seemed surprised I did not suffer jetlag after a 4,000-mile journey two days before. Even now at the age of seventy-nine I can still travel by air to Canada without suffering the jetlag so talked about.

The next day which was Sunday, Eirene was not well and spent the day in bed. The servants always had Sunday off, so I cooked the dinner and washed up, but oh dear, although Joseph looked after things very well, I could not tell which was the dish-cloth, so I cut up an old tea towel to use for the dish-cloth!

In the afternoon, Richard took the children and me to an African market, where all produce, wares and materials were simply spread on the grass. The dried fish smelled horrible. We were the only whites to be seen. Much to my surprise, we were followed everywhere we went by the African children, all wanting to shake hands. Peta, who was a true blonde, caused quite a stir. She received many admiring stares from people of all ages. No wonder, for she was the only fair person in the market. Carolyn, like her father, was black-haired, with a skin tanned to near brown. The locals did not even glance her way.

After we had looked all round the market, we went to see Joseph and his mother in their shack, which was rather above average for an African home, but goodness me, we could smell the place twenty yards before we reached it! Joseph's mother asked us in. The place had no windows, a mud floor, with a few pictures hanging on the mud walls. The furniture consisted of home-made rustic chairs and a form. The lady fondled my pearls and pointing to her ugly home-made beads, started jabbering in Swahili. Of course, I could not understand one word, so I asked Joseph to translate all she said. Apparently she wanted me to exchange my pearls for her home-made beads. Then she said to Richard: "How old is your mother?" When he told her I was seventy years old on the next day, she exclaimed: "No! No! If she is seventy years old tomorrow, she should not have a straight back." Bending herself nearly double, she demonstrated how I should look and how I should walk. I longed to get away from this place, it smelled so horrible, nearly as bad as the market.

One day Eirene took me to visit the

Catholic Mission Hospital which, in the four years since it had been in Kenya, had grown from one small building to a complex that took over an hour to walk around. I saw things in that hospital the like of which I had never seen before. One two and a half-year-old boy had been admitted with malnutrition. He weighed only seven pounds, the average weight of a new-born baby. The father sat by his child who had only a few hours to live. The premature babies were in a small ward. One weighed only two and a half pounds. None looked to have any life at all. The flies were terrible, crawling all over the faces of these children, who were too ill to stop them creeping up their nostrils and into the corners of their eyes. I felt sad and sickened by the sights we saw, although we realized that those nurses and only one doctor were doing all they possibly could. The doctor was Dutch and he operated in a theatre most English doctors would refuse to work in. One saw in this hospital complete dedication.

This doctor, his wife and his baby had been involved in a car crash which seriously damaged the child's brain. Even when she was three years old, she could not walk without help. She was such a beautiful child one could not help loving her.

During the first week Eirene took me to visit two of her friends, Sue and Mairead, who came from England and Ireland to teach in a bush school. They volunteered to do this for two years. Mairead was near the end of her term and was going home at the end of that month. We found everything extremely primitive, just the bare necessities. The house had mud floors, but like all other white women these girls had a house-boy. They had a new school building, but the money had run out, so they had to wait until money was available before they could furnish it. Their toilet was just a hole in the ground, with two stones for the feet, and a temporary cover which was moved when a fresh hole was dug. These girls took everything in their stride, travelling on the local buses full of sweating Kenyans, with every kind of goods — mattresses, old bikes, furniture, and produce — piled on the top. All the buses I saw were absolutely loaded to their full capacity, and their speed was downright dangerous; they swayed from side to side in a most alarming manner. They also caused a dreadful dust, so that when a car needed to pass, the driver could not see the oncoming traffic. Richard said this caused more head-on collisions than anything else.

We visited the town of Kisumu fifty miles from Mumias. I was still looking for a doll in national costume, but again I was unlucky.

24

My Seventieth Birthday
and Our Visit to Treetops

JANUARY 8th 1977 was my seventieth birthday, which I shall never forget if I live to be a hundred. Richard and Eirene said they had arranged a dinner party in my honour, inviting around twenty guests. Their kindness in helping to make this a memorable occasion was something out of this world. Joseph plucked, dressed and cooked a turkey the day before. Eirene made bread, and I noticed several pounds of butter in the fridge, but nothing else was to be seen. "Umph!" I thought, "turkey sandwiches only." How wrong I was! The first guest to arrive, named Carolyn, was loaded with a cooked leg of pork. Then back she went to her car, returning with two huge iced cakes made in the figures of seven and naught. One guest brought bowls of salad, another a huge bowl of new teeny-weeny potatoes beautifully garnished. And so they came, nearly all bringing their contribution, until the table groaned with the good things they had taken so much trouble to make. Trifles, cakes and pastries were decorated with lashings of cream. Food was followed by a land rover bringing china, cutlery and chairs from the club. Those guests who had not made anything brought gifts. I could not possibly remember all their names, but they made me feel like a queen. After this sumptuous meal we danced and played games.

Most of the people who attended the party invited me to their homes. Jill and Peter Brown were especially kind. I will always remember their hospitality. They had two boys, Mathew and Daniel, who were great friends with Ricky, and a wee girl named Olivia. Then there were John and Carolyn, who were very good friends of Richard and Eirene. They had a baby called Rebecca. Sad to relate, John died in Kenya, having contracted hepatitis. I also like to remember Di and Stuart Hayes. We had dinner at their place to meet Stuart's parents who were also on holiday in Kenya.

During my time there the sugar company held its annual sports day for the workers. I was invited to watch these sports which took place in terrific heat. Very few white people ventured out. I was lucky to be sitting with the boss and his wife underneath the shade of a bamboo shelter. We came to no harm from the sun, but Richard, who was helping to organize the sports, was quite severely sunburned, even though he was used to the hot climate. The sports, even though I did not know any of the participants, were really entertaining. The grace of some of those young Kenyans was a joy to watch.

By this time my holiday in Kenya was half over. One of the best trips, which was a birthday present from Richard and Eirene, was still to come — a visit to Treetops and to Lord Baden-Powell's cottage. Treetops was where Princess Elizabeth heard the sad news of the death of her father, George VI, which made her Queen of England. Lord Baden-Powell's cottage is a popular expedition for people visiting Treetops.

305

It was built for him on his retirement as Chief Scout. He had fallen in love with that part of Kenya during his attendance at rallies which took place throughout the country. He loved the wonderful views over the plains and the twin peaks of Mount Kenya, named Batian and Nelion, which are always snow-clad though straddling the equator. Pieces of Baden-Powell's furniture remain in the cottage, and some of his many books are on display there. Preserved now in his memory, the cottage, named "Paxto", has been redecorated internally in the scout colours of blue and gold. I was glad to have seen the cottage where that great man spent the last few years of his life. He died on January 8th 1941, when he was nearly 84 years old.

We arose early for this over 300-mile journey which we hoped to do in one day, in spite of the potholes and bumps we would encounter. When we had travelled about fifty miles, Richard asked me if everything looked misty. I answered: "Not more than usual." After a while he complained that his contact lenses had started to hurt him. When he stopped the car for petrol, he took this opportunity to put some comfy drops in his eyes, but the further we went, the worse his eyes became.

We stopped in Nukuru for coffee and sandwiches. On the pathway outside the cafe were a lot of carved animals and African pottery. I spent more time looking at these than Richard thought I ought, but I cannot resist looking at these beautifully carved animals. After a lot of bargaining, I bought a few, then we were on our way again.

The next stop was Thompson's Falls. I was disappointed in these falls: the scenery was glorious, but compared with the spectacular Niagara Falls in Canada, Thompson Falls were a mere trickle. It was at Thompson Falls Hotel that I changed twenty pounds in travellers' cheques. I was disgusted with the 13/6 I received per pound. I felt I had been diddled, for in Nairobi I had received 14/6. English currency was really low during that year (1977). When I changed this money, the receptionist jeered at our low currency; I could have slapped his face. At the Thompsons Falls shop

I bought more of the carved animals, surprisingly much cheaper than those on the footpath in Nukuru.

By this time Richard was becoming quite worried about his eyes, and when we reached the Out Span Hotel, where we spent the night prior to our visit to Treetops, he was seeing rainbow colours round all the lights. He took out his contact lenses, and put on his glasses, but this made no difference. By this time we were both extremely worried, so the next morning we asked the hotel receptionist if she could recommend a good doctor. She told us the name of their own doctor and then she drew a map to enable us to find his surgery. We travelled a few miles to this town called Nyeri, but found the doctor did not attend surgery on Sundays. They recommended another doctor who also was out. We walked around a bit and at last saw another doctor's name-plate. Only one other person was in the surgery, a poorly-dressed black woman. Although she was there before us, the doctor pushed her on one side, and beckoned us into his surgery. We felt awful about this, as in England this would never happen. The doctor made a great show of examining Richard's eyes, then told him he had conjunctivitis. He gave him some drops, and said "One hundred and twenty shillings, please." That was an awful lot of money in those days. Richard said: "Oh my goodness! That's a bit steep, isn't it?" He took off ten shillings and gave Richard a receipt. Richard whispered: "Mother, you look too smartly dressed. He has grossly over-charged us."

We had our midday meal at the Out Span, which was one of the most beautiful hotels I had ever seen. It stood in several acres of ground, with the most lovely gardens, a river for fishing, and a golf-course nearby. At three o'clock three mini-buses called to take us to Treetops, which I found much more primitive than I had expected. We were taken by the warden across the forest and were told to keep behind him in case we met a wild animal. He carried a gun, so we were not too alarmed. When we came in sight of Treetops, I thought: "No wonder they called it by that name,"

for it is literally built round a huge tree. This Treetops was not the first one, where the young Princess Elizabeth stayed in 1952 with her husband Prince Philip. That one was much smaller and had been burnt down.

We were taken up on to the roof, where we were given tea, hot scones, sandwich-cake, and pineapple on forks. We did not see many wild animals at the huge water-hole until after the dark hour, but the baboons were very entertaining. We were warned by the warden that we must never leave our bedroom windows open, as the baboons had been known to climb the walls and enter a bedroom, causing havoc by tearing up the bed clothes and the guests' garments, even ripping open handbags and chewing everything within. These baboons were of every size: mothers with young, and one the warden called Grandma, whom he had known for twenty-five years. He kept pocketsful of biscuits which he gave them in turn. When they had eaten all the biscuits, all the baboons but Grandma disappeared as if by magic. We were looking over the guard-rails when suddenly I noticed a baboon climbing the wall where the kitchens were situated. I nudged Richard and pointed to this baboon who by that time was crawling into the kitchen through an open window. In seconds he was out again with a bag of buns. Then pandemonium broke out. Every baboon raced to the scene, fighting and scratching to tear open the strong polythene bag of buns. When all the buns were eaten, peace reigned once more, but all the visitors stayed where they had watched this play, until another baboon climbed into the kitchen, coming out this time with a sliced loaf. Then the fun started all over again. Richard and I both thought this window was purposely left open in order to provide entertainment for the visitors. Those baboons raced up the walls, jumping the guard-rails faster than the eye could follow. As I stood against the rails, a baboon out of the blue suddenly jumped over my shoulder. I never saw anything so quick.

We then went down to an extremely good dinner, after which the floodlights were turned on the water-hole, and we all found a position where we could watch the wild animals coming in for their evening drink. That night we saw around two hundred buffalos, thirty elephants, two rhinos and numerous warthogs, wild cats and mongoose. The antelopes were very timid but beautiful. No lions or leopards appeared that night, but we heard the hyenas fighting.

Richard and I shared a very small bedroom, so small we could reach out and touch each other, as there were only two feet between the bunk-type beds fitted up to the wall. By this time Richard's eyes were becoming much worse and he was dreading the 300 miles driving home, but he would not allow me to drive. The drops were useless, and after we were all taken back to the Out Span for breakfast, we set off home to Mumias. We arrived home without incident, and the next morning Richard went to his own doctor who asked him if he still had his contact lenses in. When he answered: "Definitely no," the doctor said it looked as though he had. After five days of mistiness and pain, he asked Eirene to put some drops in his eyes.

She screamed out: "Richard, you have my contact lenses in your eyes!" And he had! Eirene had mistakenly put her lenses in Richard's steriliser, and he had then put his own on top of hers. The two sets of lenses had stuck together, and Richard had put both in his eyes. When he had tried to remove them, only his own set had come out, leaving Eirene's in. No wonder everything looked misty. Richard arranged to see a specialist optician in Nairobi to make sure he had not received any permanent damage to his eyes through lack of oxygen.

The saddest day of my holiday was when Eirene and I went to see little Madeleine's grave. The baby was buried in a very small cemetery which was cut out of the bush and, owing to the rapid growth of foliage in Kenya, was quickly going back to bush. Cows were grazing in the cemetery. Madeleine's grave was the only one with a little cross and the only one that was cared for. Eirene had taken a beautiful spray of red and white bougainvilleas which she had made herself. Looking at that tiny grave I felt sad, and wished I had known her, but I was glad to be with Eirene that day. The poignancy of standing together saying a little prayer — mine was for the child's mother to be given strength to bear such a loss — was heartbreaking.

25

Travelling in Kenya

WHENEVER one travels in Mumias, one sees numerous lorryloads of sugar cane coming in from all directions, with huge trailers behind, all making their way to the sugar-cane factory which, I was told, turned out twenty lorryloads of refined sugar each working day. I was sorry not to have seen inside the sugar factory. I often wish I had made more effort, but time passed so quickly. I did not realize that, before harvesting the cane, they set fire to it. Every evening for miles around one could see the different plantations burning merrily. They lit up the sky. The next morning the Kenyan workers could be seen chopping down the cane where the fires had burned the previous night. Looking at those blackened sticks, one wondered where they got the sugar from.

One day when Eirene and I were motoring along the air-strip she suddenly stopped the car, jumped out and ran along the air-strip and into the sugar-cane, where she started pulling the few sugar-cane flowers, which are very beautiful and much sought after for house decoration by the white women in the compound. These flowers are supposed to give people the flu, so they lacquer them several times for safety. Not many people believe this story, but still they keep on with the spraying.

By this time our life in Kenya had settled into a definite pattern. The children used to wake very early. Ricky was always first out of bed. He would creep very quickly to my room, and almost silently open my door, then he would peep in to see if I was awake. Sometimes I pretended to be asleep, and he would quietly close the door and squat down outside the door for about ten minutes or so and then have another peep. If I was awake, he would give me a most beautiful smile, but would always wait for me to say: "Come in." He was usually armed with a game of scrabble. Then he would climb into my bed, open up the board, and we would start our game. Sometimes it was only six o'clock in the morning. We hardly ever finished this game, because the girls woke up and came bounding into the room, jumping all over the bed, crying: "Tell us a story, Grandma, about when you were a little girl." Ricky always took this very well indeed, but I thought it a pity to spoil a game half way through, especially one morning when he was beating me soundly, and young Peta just knocked the board for six all over the bed. I tried hard to replace all the counters, but found it impossible.

After that catastrophe we made an agreement to take turns: one morning a game for Ricky, and the next morning stories for the girls. Ricky always chose a game of scrabble or reversi. Carolyn sometimes chose a game of Sorry. Poor little Carolyn could not bear to lose at this game. She would first start to pout, and as the game went against her, she got more and more upset and worried. Then suddenly she would upset the board completely. After a quiet talk with her about being a good sport, she would be much better for a while, but bless her, how she hated losing. Peta would always choose a story. She would say: "I want to hear about The Three Bears", and would not be content until she had cleared the other two to the outside of the bed, and she cuddled under the clothes with me. Peta is certainly a child that knows her own mind and sticks to it.

When Mairead came to stay, she brought Ricky her own game of Travel Scrabble. He was so pleased with this, because the letters were so firmly fixed in the perforated board even the boisterous Peta could not dislodge them. Those mornings in bed with the children are golden memories for me, and I missed them greatly on my return home, but I was compensated by my other grandchildren living in England, who stay with me quite often, and all creep into my bed with the same request: "Please tell us a story about when you were young."

The twilight in Kenya is really beautiful. The dark hour comes suddenly, then the noise of the cicadas is so deafening people sometimes cannot hear each other speak.

There was a type of tree in Kenya named jacaranda, which had a flower that was a beautiful shade of mauve. It grew to about the size of an English fully-grown standard apple-tree. On each side of the road as you enter the town of Nukuru there were mile upon mile of these trees, most of which were in full bloom. This really magnificent avenue of colour one could never forget, it made a glorious entrance to the town.

We arose early to go on our last shopping expedition to a town called Eldoret, which required a ninety-mile journey along a road which was one of the few to be tarmacked. Eirene did the ninety miles in exactly one and a half hours as there was practically no traffic so early in the morning. When we were about half way there, Eierene said: "Look out around here, as we often see giraffes in the wild, and sometimes they even cross the road." We did not see any cross the road, but we did see a number of them on each side a little way into the bush. They are so tall, we could see them over quite high trees and bushes nibbling off the trees.

On entering the town we saw bougainvilleas ablaze with colour. Eldoret was the most Europeanised town I had seen in Kenya, apart from Nairobi. Cheese-making was the main industry, but we did not have time to visit any of these factories. I was aghast at the price of a box of pins, no bigger than a match-box, for which Eirene paid 18/6. After a good look around the shops, we had lunch, then Eirene thought we should be making our way home, because she had promised Richard to be home before the dark hour which closes in suddenly in Africa.

Our journey home proved hazardous. First, we had to pass eight petrol-tankers, with huge tanker trailers behind each of them, on their way to Uganda. One could not pass these on the narrow roads until their drivers gave the signal that it would be safe to do so. When we were safely by this lot, Eirene sounded the horn as a thank you gesture and the confounded thing stuck. There we were travelling around seventy miles an hour, the horn blaring like mad. It was awful. Eirene pulled the car in, when we reached a suitable place, and she fiddled about with the steering-wheel. After a while it stopped, but unluckily by this time all the tankers had passed us again, so once again began the tortuous slow job of passing them again.

We had progressed only a few more miles, when we were stopped by police and around two hundred Africans blocking our way. After the police had made a clearway for us to pass these people, we saw to our horror that a woman had been killed in the road, and we were to see the ritual that was customary in the country of all the relatives swaying and wailing over the body. I learned that among certain Kenyan tribes, after someone had died, the relatives would wail for hours. Then the body was taken into the bush, and the wild animals carried out the work they were meant to do. These tribes do not believe in a life after death, and therefore the body was disposed of in that way. Richard and Eirene had never heard of this happening in their part of Kenya.

After this second setback I passed the remark: "I wonder if there will be a third." I am only superstitious in that one thing: when two things happen, quite often there will be a third, as has so often been the case in my life. Sure enough, we were within fifteen miles of home, when Eirene said, quite unconcerned: "Mum, we have a puncture." I said: "Oh surely not," although I knew we had by the bumping under my side of the car. We drew to the side of the road, where fortunately there was a yard or two of level grass. Eirene said: "Don't you worry, Mum. I have changed many a wheel. Richard would not let me drive all these miles if I could not." But could she heck! For a start she could not budge the spare wheel from under the back of the car. Our combined efforts of tugging and pulling proved useless.

I stood up to ease my aching shoulders and there, to my surprise, I counted thirty-nine Kenyans watching us. Talk about bush telegraph! I wondered where on earth they had sprung from in those few minutes and not a house in sight. Eirene was wearing a mini-dress, a very short mini, and there was I dodging from side to side hoping they would not see what I could see, as she bent over, trying to release that dratted spare-wheel. Several of the natives offered their help, which she refused in rather a firm voice, saying: "No, thank you, I can manage." Then a superior-looking African boy, who looked a little over twenty years old and was carrying books under his arm (I thought he might be a student or a young school-teacher) said: "May I help you, Mem Sahib?" "No, thank you," said Eirene once again, but this one took not a blind bit of notice, and began to release the spare wheel. In a matter of ten minutes he had finished the job. Eirene gave him a ten-shilling note, then we were on our way once again. I said to Eirene: "Were you a bit mean? I would have given him a pound, although he did seem delighted with ten shillings." Eirene said ten shillings were as much as he would earn in two days and he would be very happy with them. We were so relieved to be on our way again, as dark hour was approaching and Richard would be getting worried.

26

My Return Home

ON my last Saturday evening Richard and Eirene were going to a party given by Peter and Jill Brown for Michael and Penny, who were leaving Mumias to take another job with the same firm in Somalia. For this occasion Eirene decided she would like a new outfit. She had a length of white cambric which she made into a blouse. I had taken her a length of green and white material, so I set to and made her a full-length pinafore dress. She looked really lovely in this outfit.

My time in Kenya was getting short — only Sunday and Monday left before my departure on Tuesday, January 25th. We spent most of this time together at home, with the odd visit to the club to say our goodbyes and to the Browns for dinner.

We started out on the Tuesday

morning around eleven o'clock, bound for Nairobi. I was so sad to leave them, and I felt Eirene looked poorly and was as upset as I was at the parting, knowing it would be a long time before we saw each other again. Our journey to Nairobi was uneventful. Richard drove well and we made very good progress.

Richard took me to his hotel, where he had made an arrangement to stay a few nights, as he had to interview students for positions at the Mumias factory. My plane did not leave until midnight, so I was staying in Richard's room with him until the time of my departure for the airport. A phone-call came to his room, enquiring why a lady was there with him with luggage, when he had only booked for one gentleman. Richard was highly amused at this, and after pulling their leg a bit, told them he had his mother with him until he took her to the airport at midnight, and asked if they had any objection. They apologised profusely, saying that would be quite alright. After Richard had rested a while, we went out for a walk round a Nairobi park. Unfortunately we had only gone a few yards when the cartilage in my right knee slipped out as I stepped off the curb, making me as lame as a cat. We walked a short distance into the park, but the pain was so excruciating we had to return to the hotel.

At eight o'clock Richard took me to the Norfolk Hotel for dinner. (I read in the newspaper recently that this beautiful hotel had been burnt to the ground, and that arson was suspected.) Here we were to meet Jill Brown and her friend Kath, who were in Nairobi to buy a present for Michael and Penny before they left for Somalia. Over one hundred pounds had been collected in Mumias towards this present, a sure sign of how well they were liked and respected. Although it was late at night and quite dark, we partook of this dinner in the grounds of the hotel, under very subdued lighting. The magnificent foyer was a joy to behold, having glass cases containing the most beautiful ivory carvings I have ever seen, from tiny ones to a whole tusk carved into the shape of a Viking ship, costing hundreds of pounds. I enjoyed so much that hour spent looking at these carvings and the lovely feather flowers that were made by cripples who, when the flamingoes were moulting, used to go to the lakeside to gather up their feathers, some of which were bleached white for bridal bouquets, some dyed green for leaves, and others brown for the stalks. Richard and Eirene gave me a nosegay which I wear at weddings and special occasions. This flower is admired wherever I go.

We said our goodbyes to Jill and Kath, then made our way back to Richard's hotel, and made ready to leave for the airport which was twelve miles outside Nairobi. Richard was tired after such a long day, so I asked him not to wait with me until my plane came. I was glad he did not, because the plane I was booked on was full, and fourteen of us had to wait for the next plane that was due in from Somalia one hour later, and would take the rest of us to Heathrow London.

I was taken to a first-class seat, sitting against a lady a little older than myself, and who was just a little bit sub-normal, although she had moments of complete lucidity. She had travelled quite alone from south-east Africa after a six-week visit to her son. Even before I had settled myself, she grabbed my arm saying: "I'm a widow, you know. I lost my husband a year ago." Then I heard his life-story over and over again: how he was a Japanese prisoner of war, and all his illnesses until he died, what the doctor said, what her son said, and how he cried. Then would come ten minutes of real sense and sound conversation, mostly about her holiday. She told me most enjoyable stories of her stay in Africa, when suddenly she clutched hold of me and started all over again: "I am a widow, you know, etc." After over ten repeats, I pretended to be asleep, so she immediately turned to a gentleman on her other side. He pretended he could not understand English, but when she went to the washroom, he spoke perfect English to me. He was Swedish.

When we dined on the plane, she ate little, but stored all she could in her hold-all. She said: "I can eat this when I get home." As we landed at Heathrow, we saw a close-up view of Concorde.

What a lovely graceful plane it is!

When we disembarked, I was landed with this lady right up to Victoria bus station. I looked after her luggage while she found a trolley, which would not wheel straight. We caused great amusement trying to push this monster along the long, long way to customs and to terminal 3. My knee was hurting like mad, as we manoeuvred this drunken creature to our waiting bus. After we were settled in the bus, the lady started again, but I pretended to go to sleep, so she got hold of the lady across the gangway, and started her sorry tale once again. The lady seemed quite interested the first time of hearing, but she soon tired, and she also pretended to sleep. Then, thank goodness, the lady went to sleep herself, and I was able to look at London as we travelled along.

On arriving at Victoria, I helped her get a taxi, and much to my chagrin, found I had missed my bus to the Midlands by ten minutes. I had to wait several hours before the next one. I had mixed feelings about that old lady. I had to pay for my luggage to be held, while I found a restaurant where I could both eat and sit down, for by this time my knee was hurting something rotten, so I sat there all that time until nearly the time of my bus departure. At last we were on our way, and how pleased I was to take a taxi at Loughborough and to be only fifteen minutes away from home.

But oh dear! What did I find as I unlocked my front door? The fitted carpet was hanging over most of my chairs, absolutely wet through. Apparently the firm I had employed to drain the whole system — when I left we were having exceedingly hard frosts — had left the stop-tap running, when they had turned the water back on. The kitchen carpet square was found floating on four inches of water when Lizbeth came home from market, and water was pouring into the hall. She rang Michael who understood the system and soon turned off the fast-running tap.

I was fully insured, as was the plumber, who denied any responsibility. He even sent me a bill for nearly £20, which I ignored. He sent a second, and even a third, so I got on the phone and told him

I was not going to pay him for flooding my home. He denied responsibility once again, saying the cause of the trouble had been a perished washer. I told him I did not profess to know much about plumbing, but that he knew as well as I did that a tap with a worn washer did not start to pour out water to flood a house as suddenly as that, but began with a drip that gradually became worse. Then he threatened me with court proceedings, so I told him I would welcome that, but it would do more harm to his reputation as a plumber to have this story in all the local papers. "Oh!" he said, "Forget it!", which I promptly did. That tap was turned off to stop it running and still has the same washer nine years later. The insurance allowed me half the price of a new carpet square for the kitchen, and paid for a specialist to clean and re-lay the hall carpet, and stretch it back to fit up to the walls once again.

I did not worry unduly about the flooding, because I was so happy to be home again, to find everything had gone well with our egg business and with the hens, and to enjoy the many happy thoughts and memories of my month in Kenya with Richard and his family. After I had been home a few weeks, I switched on my television set, and there was a picture of the Great Rift Valley which I instantly recognized. I was very interested in the story about the natives that lived and worked there.

27

My Friends the Jalland Family

AFTER my lazy life in Kenya, I now had to settle down to work on our poultry farm. My friend Susan Jalland and her son Tim had managed the place wonderfully well with considerable help from Michael. Tim also had a friend, Peter Shaw, who helped in feeding the birds.

My friendship with the Jalland family has deepened over the years. Susan is like a second daughter to me. While working together, we relate stories of our past, receiving a lot of pleasure from them. During one of my stories Susan said: "You really should write a book." From that time I dallied with the thought that I might, then Ingrid, one of my Canadian grandchildren, said to me: "Please write these stories down, Grandma, so we will have them when you are dead." I thought to myself: "Yes!

I seem able to tell stories, but having left school at the age of thirteen years of age, I shall not be clever enough to put these stories together and write them down."

Then on one of my visits to Canada with David and his family, I was invited to a dinner-party given by a colleague of David and his wife. When I accepted this kind invitation, I was afraid I would be like a fish out of water, or at least out of my element with all those highly-educated people. Strange to say, I was not, and I never enjoyed an evening more. After a lovely dinner, we sat in a circle out on the lawn, chattering about all sorts of things, when one of the professors said how they were enjoying the James Herriot films on television. I said they were popular in England, but I could think of many stories that really happened on our farm that would have added interest to his farm stories. This gentleman, who had been to England during the war with the Canadian Air Force, and whose father had been a vicar in an English country village, said: "Tell us a few of them, Mrs. Smith."

I felt a bit shy, but I always loved

telling these stories, so I started and soon lost myself as I progressed, just as I do when telling these stories to my grandchildren. All the stories I told that night in Canada have now been written in one or another of my books. When we said our goodbyes that night, the gentleman who asked me to tell those stories took me by both arms and said: "I do not know when I enjoyed an evening more. Thank you very much." I felt a bit overwhelmed at the time, but I thought a lot about it during the next few months, thinking to myself: "If people as highly educated as they were liked my stories, perhaps I could write the book my grandchildren and my dear friend Susan Jalland are always advising me to do." I have to thank them, along with my son David, for the joy this writing has given me and their steadfast encouragement and advice.

I think and look back at the slender chance that brought me and the Jallands together. It happened like this. First, her son Tim, who was in his very early teens, came on trial to help on our poultry farm. One Saturday, while I was away at my market-stall, he came to collect the eggs. But oh dear! when I came home and saw the heap of smashed eggs at the bottom of the steps outside one of our poultry houses, I exclaimed: "Good gracious me! Whatever has happened here?" Lizbeth said: "Timmie did it, all fifteen dozen of them." She said the bottom tray disintegrated, and he dropped the lot. "Well!" I said to Lizbeth, "we just cannot have a lad work for us who cannot gather eggs without dropping that number." Robin, Lizbeth's husband, said: "I should give him one more chance, because no one told him we use two trays at the bottom of that number of eggs, and I like the lad." Timmie continued to work with us at week-ends and during school holidays until he started college. Had I told him on that day of egg smashing that we could not keep him, I shudder to think just what my family would have missed in the wonderful friendship that developed over the years with the Jalland family.

Although he worked so hard in his spare time and later worked on my egg-stall all day on Saturdays, his academic achievements were outstanding. He went to the local village school, then to Humphrey Perkins School at Barrow-on-Soar, and then at the age of fourteen, a year after he started helping at the poultry farm, to Rawlins School in Quorn. He gained eight O levels and four A levels, the latter all with A marks, and went on to Imperial College, London, where he got a first-class honours degree in physics in 1981.

When Timmie started college, Carolyn, his sister, took his place. When Carolyn went to college, her brother Robert took over. And when Robert started college, his sister, Vanessa, began work on the farm, until she got a full-time job after leaving school.

As Lizbeth and I enlarged our flock, we needed a part-time regular help for around three hours each morning. I mentioned this to Timmie, who immediately said: "My mum would like a part-time job, but she suffers a little bit with asthma and the job with feathers might not suit her. May I run home and ask her?" I said: "Of course, you may. Off you go." The Jallands live only a few hundred yards away, so he was back in a matter of minutes, saying: "Mum would very much like to try it." Fortunately the job suited her, and so started the friendship between us that has been a joy for the last ten years.

When Robin and Lizbeth found their three stalls in Nottingham were proving more than they could manage, Ivor Jalland, Susan's husband, came to work with us full-time. Ivor can put his hand to any job on the farm. He does so many things for which in the past we needed to call in a specialist. We wonder how in the wide world we ever managed without him. Numerous maintenance jobs, even fixing a new roof on a poultry house, come easy to him, and he always has such a pleasant manner. He works the whole day on Saturday at my Loughborough egg-stall, which enables me to go home around one o'clock. The only snag is when the whole Jalland family go away together, we are all at sea, we miss them so much.

Susan was the chief friend who encouraged me in the writing of my books about country folk. Often when I was relating one of my childhood stories, she would say: "That one must be written in your book." But when I sat down that same evening to write more of the book, I would have clean forgotten the story we were talking about. I remedied this by writing a few words on the grading-room walls in chalk, then entering them in what I called my rough book.

Many people who have read my books have passed the remark: "You must have kept a wonderful diary." When I tell them I have never kept a diary in my life, they can hardly believe me. Although I can so vividly remember things that happened when I was a child, I find difficulty in remembering many things that have happened recently. I am told that is one of the conditions of growing old. When I was asked to take the part of a cantankerous old village character in one of Joan Duce's plays, I found great difficulty in learning my role. When I was young, I could learn a ten-page monologue in two or three nights, retaining it for years, but now, oh dear! I can recite it to myself in bed, but the next morning I am struggling to remember any of it.

When I had decided to write my first book, Susan said: "I will illustrate and type it." When I asked her how much I would owe her, she smiled and said: "Nothing, of course. I will love to do this for you." I sat thinking one night: "Now what can I give Susan in appreciation for her help and encouragement to me?" when it suddenly came to me: buy her a dishwasher. I mentioned this to Ivor, her husband, who said he would do the extra wiring it would need. We kept all this a secret. Ivor would tell me that Susan kept saying: "I do not know why you are doing all this new wiring." He told her the wiring in the kitchen was getting old, and he wanted to avoid anyone getting shocks.

Ivor arranged to take Susan to the Royal Show so that day we managed to get a plumber at very short notice to fix the new dishwasher that had been previously stored at my place in the store-room. We were afraid that one day Susan would go in and see it. Every time she needed egg cartons I would say: "I will fetch them." We were lucky, for when they came home from the show at nearly midnight, and when she saw her lovely new dishwasher she could not believe her eyes. Ivor said she sat down beside it, with tears running down her face, and she kept saying: "Nothing has ever happened to me like this before." Afterwards she said to me: "But, Mrs. Smith, I have not done anything yet." I answered: "No, not yet, but this contraption will do your washing-up, while you are typing and drawing the pictures." Having four children and doing a lot of cooking, she finds it a great help, often calling it her best friend.

I shall end this chapter with a couple of stories which concern Robert Jalland, Ivor and Susan's second son. He worked for us at week-ends, as did a girl named Diane. Both were taking a course at Loughborough College and both were having driving lessons. We had a lot of fun listening to these two relating their experiences about their driving. Robert took his driving test first, coming home quite despondent, having failed. When I asked him: "What did you do wrong?"

He answered: "I stopped at the lights at red, and when they changed to green, started to move off again. Then the examiner stopped me because I had not noticed that another person had stepped on to the crossing." He said that was the only thing he did wrong. Diane came home waving her pass certificate. I congratulated her, but she said: "Mrs. Smith, I did several things wrong. I was quite sure I would fail." I laughed and told her: "It was your pretty face, and lovely smile that worked the oracle." (Robert passed the second time he took the test.) Another time Diane's smile kept her out of trouble was when she was serving dinner at the Durham Ox Hotel at Six Hills. This happened on her first time there. She was feeling a bit shy, and worried that she would not acquit herself well. She was serving peas, and was not quite able to hold the serving equipment correctly, therefore spilling the peas all over a gentleman's shoulder. Her exclamation "I am so sorry, sir, this is my first evening here." brought a smile to the gentleman's face. Then he asked her questions about her work. "Oh,"

343

she answered, "I go to Loughborough College, where I am taking a two-year course in domestic science." Diane ended up with the gentleman giving her a tip of a five-pound note. Diane has the most beautiful smile, which I feel will get her wherever she wants to go.

28

The Long Hot Summer

ON looking out of my window, I think back to the time when we first lived here. We then could see numerous majestic elm trees; now, sad to say, every one has died of the terrible Dutch elm disease. In the winter months, when work on the farm is lessened, Michael takes his saw and fells these trees one by one, sawing them into suitably sized logs for customers who still like an open fire. I was told that Dutch elm disease did not come to England from Holland, but from some elm planks that were shipped over the Atlantic, presumably from America. I do remember, when I first went over to Canada fifteen years ago, seeing their elms stark and white, with absolutely no covering of bark. When I asked the farmer what had happened to his elms, his answer was: "Oh, Dutch elm disease has killed the lot of 'em." I had never even heard of it in England, but now, having started in the south, it has crept over the whole country, leaving it absolutely bare of that most majestic tree that takes over fifty years to grow to maturity. This has been a tragedy for the beautiful English countryside.

The following poem was given to me by its author, Mr. Edward Mansell Buxton, with full permission to include it in this chapter, for which I thank him:

The power-saw screeches through
    the elm.
Oh! cheerless days are these,
As one by one we say goodbye
To England's stately trees.

It seems there's nought that man
    can do,
But just stand helpless by,
While in the woods and lanes we see
The elm trees quickly die.

And as we walk through leafy glades
In the autumnal breeze,
We murmur fervently a prayer:
God spare the other trees.

I hear that in America they now have a tree which grows and matures rapidly and is taking the place of the elm.

I have found in my garden several young sycamore trees. How they have set root there, I do not know, because there is not a sycamore in sight of my garden. Perhaps the birds or strong winds have brought the seeds. Two have grown to about six or seven feet, and they have been transplanted to a suitable place. The others will go up north to my son's place in Yorkshire where few trees have been grown.

We also have quite a number of ash trees that are also self-sown, and two cherry trees have now appeared, along with numerous hawthorn trees. Michael resets these in gaps in the hedgerows, as we cannot possibly allow them to stay in between beds of roses and summer flowers only a few yards away from the house. Country people call these self-sown trees bastards. They sure like the soil in my garden, and I just cannot destroy them until they are ready to transplant.

One kind of bastard I have welcomed

is the Cotoneaster, a beautiful tree or shrub that will cover an old wall or fence, keeps green all winter, has flowers in the summer and bunches of lovely red or yellow berries in the winter. Luckily I have had four of these.

Somehow some soils grow things quite successfully, where other soils fail completely. My own garden grows daffodils in profusion, but tulips fail after the first year. Another flower that is rampant in my garden which few others can grow is a pink lily, very seldom seen. They have up to nine or ten flowers on a very strong stem in the most delicate shade of pink, and the flower is almost like a miniature orchid. They are sometimes called Naked Ladies, as all the leaves die before they flower. Their real name is Noreen. I gathered so many one day they decorated a whole ward in a Melton Mowbray hospital, where my sister Lottie will stay for the rest of her life, suffering from Parkinson's disease. They are an exotic lily and will last in the house in a cool place for several weeks. Their bulbs are minute, but in my soil they multiply ten times in one year, and they are the envy of all my friends, who have been given bulbs from time to time, but it is always the same story: "They do not grow in my garden the way they do in yours." This year I am going to suggest they take some of my soil to see if that will help. I think they set the bulbs much too deep, as they should only be set half way into the soil, unlike daffodils that need setting several inches deep. I saw some of these lilies for sale in a shop priced 30p. each. I went home and counted mine which amounted to one hundred and eighty three, and that was after I had given many to friends. "Goodness me!" I thought, "at 30p. each I have over fifty pounds worth of lilies."

One evening during the raspberry-picking time my son Sidney said to Lizbeth: "We are going away for the weekend. Would you like to go and pick our raspberries, as it would be a shame to let them spoil?" Lizbeth was delighted to oblige, as they are her favourite of all fruits. She had been gathering for over an hour, and had gathered around four pounds, when Sidney's neighbour, Margaret Morris, called to Lizbeth: "Hi there, what are you doing gathering my raspberries?" Lizbeth was quite shaken. She said: "Of course, I am not, I am gathering our Sidney's while they are away." "Well!" says Margaret, "You're not gathering your Sidney's, you are gathering mine. Sidney's are over there." Their gardens were adjacent, without a fence between them, and although Margaret's raspberries were nearer Sidney's house, his were a few yards further on. "Oh dear!" says Lizbeth, "I shall have to give you these and start all over again." "Well," says Margaret, "I have not got any gooseberries, have you?" "Well," says Lizbeth, "I haven't, but me mam has. You can have some of those, if you like." So they made a deal: Lizbeth could keep the raspberries, if Margaret could have my gooseberries. I chuckle to myself even now when I think about this deal. I was the only loser: Lizbeth kept her raspberries and Margaret had my gooseberries. Margaret scored again, when I rang her to say I had layered some gooseberry stems which had taken root and asked if she would like them. "I would very much," answered Margaret,

and she fetched them the same day. I hoped they would grow and not die as all her other gooseberry bushes had.

We shall all remember that year of 1976, for it was the hottest summer I can ever recall. The grass was cut one day, turned the following day, and gathered in the next, making it the best hay possible. The corn harvest was poor because of lack of rain, but what there was of it was all gathered in by the end of July.

On our poultry farm we had two severe frights caused by hedgerows getting on fire. The first caught fire from a bonfire a neighbour's children had lighted in their garden. The grass around the fire was so dry the sparks ignited it, then the slight wind wafted it towards the hedge setting it alight. This fire was put out without sending for the fire brigade, but the second was much worse, and was caused, it was thought, by a cigarette being thrown from a car window. This fire was not seen until it was well alight, and was impossible to extinguish without the fire brigade. Within twenty minutes the firemen were there and soon had the fire under control. Our greatest fear was for around 2,000 birds which we were rearing for our replacement layers and whose house was a matter of several hundred yards away, and also for the two and half acres of standing corn in the next field.

Bonfires, car-washing and the watering of gardens were forbidden by law. People's lawns which stayed green were suspect. Some of them were reported and their owners were warned by the authorities to stop watering them, as the reservoirs were nearly empty.

I myself cannot stand extreme heat, and had to stop work during the afternoons, but I accomplished my work by getting up very early in the mornings, resting during the heat of the day, then working again after tea. My grandchildren, like many others, ran about stark naked all day. Their feet became so hardened, they could run across our gravel drive without hurt.

Our hens did not fare too badly. The huge electric fans were set at full speed both night and day. Even so, during the hottest part of the day the hens sat with their beaks open and their wings down. They ate much less than usual, which cost less for food, but my! the electric bill, with using those huge fans twenty-four hours a day, soared to an astronomical amount. The hens laid fewer eggs, too, so we were hit both ways.

When the first rain came, after weeks and weeks of hot sunshine, we all ran outside holding up our faces, crying: "Ahh! Ahh! Isn't this lovely?" Then we sang and danced with pleasure, bringing true the song called "Singing in the rain." The fields of grass, which had been completely brown, started to grow and look green again, and the countryside began to seem like England again instead of the desert-like appearance of the previous few months.

29

Funny Things Children Say and Do

LIZBETH'S boys, John and Richard, were growing up next door, becoming the joy of my life. Some of the lovely things they say and do are really worth writing down, so we can read once again about the innocent happenings when they were young.

John was around three or four years old, and had been gathering eggs with his cousin Brian, when he came running up to me, saying excitedly: "Grandma, guess how many eggs I have gathered today." After I had made several incorrect guesses, he exclaimed, "Over two hundred, Grandma." "Oh!" I said, "that is a lot of eggs for a little boy to gather. Did you break any?" Pulling a funny face he answered: "No, Grandma." Then I said: "Are you sure you did not break any, John?" Well he answered: "Actually, I dropped two and the floor broke them."

Ever since he came home from the hospital where he was born, young Richard was called Poz. This name has stuck, even at school. Funnily enough, he likes it better than his real name Richard. Poz was under three years old when his mother took him round a Nottingham store, where she was having a job to curb his high spirits. He was touching things he should not, and moving other things, when a lady patted him on the head saying: "My word, laddie, you are full of beans aren't you?" He gave her a dirty look and answered: "No, I'm not full of beans, I had fish, chips and peas for dinner."

One day I was having a little after-dinner rest, covered down with a shawl when Poz came rushing in, shouting: "Get your covers off, Grandma, and come on out and have a game of bowls." (We have a set of carpet bowls.) So, of course, off came my covers, and I aroused myself with a great effort, found the set of bowls, and staggered out on to the lawn, where we enjoyed an hour or so of the game the boys are so keen about at the moment. I hope that, when they grow up, they will love the real game of bowls in the way so many of their Smith relations enjoy it.

Children often get words confused. I was giving a children's party, when the kiddies wondered what game they were to play next. Poz shouted: "I know. Let's play hide and find." The other day Poz was telling me that until recently he always thought it was "No one built the ark," instead of "Noah built the ark." One day John came running into my house and said: "Mummy says: 'Would you like to come to my house for dinner?'" I answered: "Yes, please. What are you having for dinner?" "Oh," he said, "we are having stinking kidney pie."

Young John is an extremely deep thinker. It was nearing Christmas, and he had been learning at school about the birth of Jesus. On that Christmas Eve he said to me: "Grandma, I love the story about Jesus, but why did he have to die?" I felt very moved. I thought of the saying "Out of the mouths of babes and sucklings" and "A little child shall lead them." Those words of John would make the most confirmed atheist wonder.

John had been at school just a few

weeks when his mother said: "Come on, John, we must practise a few words before you go to bed." "Oh, Mummy," he answered, "I cannot practise reading tonight, my mouth is too tired."

One day John stood looking at their rather large bungalow when suddenly he said: "My Daddy must have a lot of rich to build our house, there is such a lot of bricks and mortar in it."

I love remembering the funny things my children and grandchildren have said. I hope they won't bore my readers, but as the three books I have written were really for their benefit alone, without a thought of their ever being published, I feel I must continue with the thought of my grandchildren mostly in my mind. As that is the way my mind seems to work, I shall continue this chapter of reminiscences just for them.

Brian asked one day: "Grandma, what is it you have got growing on your eyes? Is it doggaracts?" When I laughed at this, and told him: "No, not doggaracts, but cataracts", he answered: "Ah well, I knew it was an animal of some sort."

I had just had a new exhaust on my

car, which I had left on my drive for a few hours, before taking a load of eggs into Leicester. The noise from that new exhaust was enough to wake the dead. I clinked and clanked my way through Leicester, thinking the police would surely stop me. It was awful every time I stopped at the lights, and even worse when I started again. After I had unloaded around 250 dozen eggs, I made my way home again, the empty car making more noise than ever. It was a relief to be back again. I got on the phone and, I must admit, was quite sharp with the owner of the garage who had fixed the new exhaust. He said: "I cannot think what has gone wrong, but bring it straight in and I will have a look at it. I really am sorry about this." I took the car and left it at the garage. After a few hours, I received a telephone call saying: "Fetch your car, Mrs. Smith. We dismantled the exhaust, which was filled with stones from off your drive." Young Poz had noticed the shiny new exhaust and had enjoyed filling it with stones. Then it was my turn to apologize to the garage owner.

Julia, Michael's daughter, became very excited when she learned that her Grandma Gamble was giving her a pony named Easter Boy to be shared by her two girl grandchildren. Julia loved this pony, and when her cousin Amanda decided to sell her share to Julia, her joy knew no bounds. This horse was completely white. Julia became an elegant rider. I love to look out of my window and watch her gallop around my field. Now she has fixed up small jumps, and is doing quite well.

Julia was serving eggs at the farmhouse door when her customer asked if she had any cracked ones and was told: "Sorry we have not got any cracked ones." In a bit of fun but with a serious face the customer said: "You better crack a few for me then." Childlike she went back and cracked half a dozen for him, charging the low price for cracked eggs. Since she has grown older, she often tells this story to her young cousins, advising them not to be caught out as she was.

A lovely story I remember so well was when my grandson Ricky was staying with me. He would then have been around ten years old. Along with his younger sisters he arrived home after a walk in the fields surrounding my bungalow. In his hand was a bunch of wild oats which he presented to me with a kind of embarrassed look on his face. Bless him, I arranged the wild oats in a tall glass vase, and put them on my kitchen window sill, and there they still reside where I can see them nearly all the time.

Another gift came from two of my youngest grandchildren, John and Poz. They came in, looking a bit sheepish; John gave me a five-pence piece, and Poz gave me one penny. They must have heard someone talking about my book, Seven Pennies in My Hand. I still have those two coins.

My youngest granddaughter, Beth, is very forward for her age of four years. During one Christmas-time she went to a service where she heard Jesus was everywhere. When she came home, she told her family that Jesus was to the right of her, Jesus was to the left of her, Jesus was up there (pointing to the ceiling) and Jesus was down there (pointing to the floor). Then she added: "And I am sitting on his lap!"

Another time I was playing snap with Hannah and Beth. Their great-auntie Edna was telling them that, when we were young, I used to cheat, picking up the cards whether I said snap first or not. Young Beth must have listened carefully to this, because when she was nearly out of her cards, and there was a sizeable number of cards on the table, like lightning she picked up the cards, saying: "I said snap first but no one heard me." The young monkey had not said one word.

One very wet day Hannah was watching television when they gave out: "This is the News Summary." In a very disgusted voice Hannah said: "Well, I don't think much to his summery weather."

I also remember a few of my own children's sayings and doings. When Sidney was very small he mixed f with s. He would say: "Setch my flippers, Mummy", "The fun is fhining in the fhy", and "Seel this, Mummy, it seels foft."

One day he got hold of my brand-new

362

enamel ladle and was banging it on our old brick floor. I shouted: "No, no, Sidney, don't bang my nice new ladle on the floor, you will make it run." "What!" he exclaimed, "Wike this?" Then he ran round the kitchen table. He thought that was what the ladle would do.

David's funniest mistake arose because he could not for the life of him say an s to which he always added an h. One day he put the four kitchen dining chairs in a row. Then he picked up one by one his five toy animals and started to place them, saying: "Doggie, you shit in that chair. Teddy, you shit in that chair. Panda, you shit in that chair. Golly, you shit in that chair." Having one more toy and no more chairs, he said: "I don't know where you're going to shit, Pussy. Ah, I know. Pussy, you can shit in the shitting room."

When Michael first saw the sea at Morecambe he cried: "Oh Mummy, what a big big bath!" Michael could not say an l. He always called himself "a tittle tad." But he knew quite well when I mocked him. He used to say: "Mummy, you said that wrong, it's not tad, it's tad!" He tried so hard to say "lad" but could not. He was nicknamed "Tad", which stuck to him all through his school days and after.

Once when my twins, Richard and Lizbeth, were two and a half years old, they were suffering from bad colds and had to be kept indoors. But on the third day the sun was shining, and it was quite warm, so I said to them: "I am going to put you both in your pram, and get you some fresh air." I took them a nice long walk, which we all enjoyed, but when we were coming back into the farmyard, Richard said: "Mummy, you didn't take us to Mr. Brown's." I was puzzled at this, as I had not mentioned going to any Mr. Brown's. "Oh! but you did, Mummy," said Richard. "You said you were going to get us some fresh hair." Then the penny dropped — Mr. Brown was the village hairdresser, and Richard thought he was going to have some new hair.

When Lizbeth started school, her teacher came to see me. She asked if I had sent money by Lizbeth to school to buy each child an ice-cream. "No, I have not," I answered. So she gave me back a right good handful of coins. I counted them up and it amounted to exactly the same money that Michael had been given for his birthday a few days before. Young Lizbeth had taken the lot to buy each child an ice cream.

A grandchild of one of my friends saw something crawling on her foot. "Grandma", he shouted, "what is that crawling on your foot?" "Oh," she answered, "that is a beatle." In great surprise he asked: "Can it sing, Grandma?" This happened during the heyday of the singing group called the Beatles.

30

A Mini-Cruise on the Q.E.2

I AM a home-loving sort of person. Since the death of my husband I have rarely left my home, apart from visiting David and his family in Canada, and Richard's while he was working in Kenya. But one day in the middle of October 1981 Michael came to see me with a secretive smile on his face. He sat down, talking about various subjects, until I began to wonder just what he had really come to talk about. Suddenly he said: "Have you seen the advert about the Q.E.2?" I answered: "No, what about her?" "Well," he drawled, piling on the suspense, "on November 24th she goes on a mini-cruise from Southampton." Michael knew one of the things I would love to do was to have a cruise on that beautiful liner, so I jumped at the chance of three days and three nights on the most fabulous ship in the world.

Michael and his wife Helen immediately made all the necessary arrangements, and my friends the Jalland family encouraged me to go. Although my hens were in full production, producing around five thousand eggs each day, the Jallands insisted they could manage. I was really eager to take advantage of this offer, even though I knew that, with both Michael and me away at the same time, the Jallands would be stretched to the limit.

When the great day arrived, Michael and Helen called for me at eight o'clock in the morning, and we set off for Southampton. We had a lovely journey, the sun was shining all the way, and we ate our sandwiches while travelling. We arrived at Southampton in exactly three and a half hours, which was good going. On arrival our luggage was taken away. We did not see it again until it was in our cabins. A firm called Andrews took charge of the car, which they brought back on our return. Everything seemed to be made extremely easy for us.

I shall never forget that first sight of the majestic Q.E.2. I expected it to be big, but not that big. There were 1,800 passengers and 900 crew and staff. We found our own way to our cabins. I was relieved to find mine next door to Michael and Helen's. My cabin had a single bed, a dressing table, a fitted wardrobe and a mirror reaching from floor to ceiling. The floor was fitted with a silver-grey carpet, and much to my delight, I had a shower and toilet all to myself. Michael and Helen's was the same, but with two single beds.

First we found our way up and beyond the cabins to the stern of the ship. The sun was still shining, and we had a grand view over the water. This part of the deck was littered with builders' refuse left from the complete re-equipment of the ship. Wood, plaster, cardboard, paper, bits of carpet, were piled high in heaps. We were surprised to see all this mess, but after we were out to sea, it was all thrown overboard. The next morning the deck was scrubbed and looked immaculate.

We stayed on deck to watch the tugs easing this floating palace out of dock. Everything seemed to be moving in slow motion and after we were well and truly at sea, we made our way back to our cabins, where we found our luggage had been delivered. We unpacked and made ready for our first dinner on the Q.E.2. We climbed up ten staircases in preference to taking the lift. This way we saw much more of the ship. We realized when we were nearing the restaurant, because more and more people were coming from all directions, all making for the same place.

The restaurant was huge, beautifully appointed, with plenty of space between each table. There was no rushing, just a leisurely look around to find your own table, where we were served a seven-course dinner. We had only eaten sandwiches in the car since breakfast, so we were well and truly ready for such a feast. In subsequent meals we had to miss several courses, we were fed so well and so often.

Our meal schedule was as follows. After a huge breakfast from numerous choices, we were given coffee around eleven. Next came a seven-course luncheon. Then at four o'clock tea and cakes were served in both lounges. Last but not least came that seven-course dinner once again. Early morning tea was served on request at no extra charge.

Our daily routine varied little. After breakfast we walked about trying to see as much as possible of this magnificent ship which seemed to us the size of our village. We found seven bars in various parts of the ship, a casino and a theatre used for both film shows and concerts. There were first-class and second-class restaurants, although it was said that exactly the same food was served in each. On one of the top floors, surrounding a huge lounge called The Double Room, were the shops, where one could buy jewellery, clothes of every description, even sportswear. The shop which attracted me most was where you could buy the most lovely china, cut glass and pottery. We wondered what happened in a storm at sea. Did they have to take all those beautiful breakable articles down and pack them away? They looked just the same as they do in shops on land, with no extra fixtures for safety.

The Double Room was the place where we spent much of our time. It reached to each side of the ship. One entered by the main stairway carpeted in a lovely maroon shade, matching the upholstery in the room. Numerous armchairs and settees surrounded the polished floor, used every evening for dancing. For every two armchairs and one settee there was a long polished table where tea and cakes were served.

The Queen's Room, the most beautiful and luxurious, was furnished with putty-coloured hide armchairs, and was carpeted in a lovely shade of green. This room also reached to each side of the ship with a space in the middle for dancing. Each side was glass, so we could see other boats and ships passing by on one side and on the other the south coast of England, from Southampton to Land's End. A running commentary was enjoyed by the people watching the coastline.

Those who wanted to read had the choice of two libraries but I only read when I was in bed, because there was so much to occupy one's time, and so much to see. We were very interested in watching the players in the casino. One woman lost £150 in less than half an hour. We saw the same lady next day playing bingo. She had a black eye, so one could not help but wonder if her husband had been so cross with her for betting and losing so much money, he had landed her a good 'un.

Twice during our cruise I was sitting alone. The first time a young lady came and sat beside me, asking if I was alone. She stayed chatting until Michael and Helen appeared. The second time Michael and Helen were dancing, when a young man asked if I was alone. We chattered about many things, especially about dancing and my work with the Wymeswold Youth Fellowship, where Sid and I had taught the teenagers of our village how to dance. When Michael and Helen had finished their dance, they said we looked so immersed in our conversation, they left us to it, while they went for a drink, fetching me later. I learned afterwards that this lady and gentleman were husband and wife and it was their job to seek out people who were alone and talk with them. They also gave dancing lessons each afternoon which they invited me to attend.

A quiz show organized by one of the

passengers was much enjoyed. We heard afterwards that he had been offered a free trip on the Queen on her next long cruise, if he would take charge of the same kind of quiz game. Needless to say, he accepted with pleasure. The quiz show was followed by games of bingo. One person won £102.

The last evening was a gala night. All the men were given a straw boater and the ladies a silver headband, with a green ostrich feather reminiscent of The Roaring Twenties. When a competition for the Charleston was announced, I was dancing with Michael. What did he do? Left me flat on my own, because he could not do it. I loved this crazy dance of the twenties and although I was then seventy-four years old, I could still do it, because every time a Charleston tune came on the wireless or television, I always got up and had a go. So although Michael left the floor, I stayed and danced it on my own, as did many others.

Also on that last evening all the passengers were invited to drink with the captain in the Queen's Room.

Champagne was there in abundance. Whenever one's glass became empty, it was immediately filled up again. I saw one lady sitting next to us drink eight full glasses. I could only manage two.

There was a beauty competition, and every girl who entered was given a parasol as a memento. Only a small number entered the competition for the most glamorous grandma. One grandma looked only in her middle thirties, but she did not win anything. The third prize was won by a beautifully dressed old lady who had five grandchildren, and five great-grandchildren. Believe me, she was really glamorous. I thought she would win the competition.

I went to bed that last evening thinking how lucky I was that at long last my dream of a cruise on the Q.E.2 had been realized.

31

Sad Times for My Wootton Family

LITTLE did I know during my cruise that a very sad time was coming for my Wootton family. My brother John, youngest but one in my family of three brothers and three sisters, went on an extended tour of America and Canada, along with some of his late wife's relatives. He came home absolutely full of praise for his "holiday of a lifetime", as he called it, but "Oh dear!" he said, "How tired I am!"

We all put this tiredness down to the amount of travelling he had done, but instead of getting over it, he became gradually worse. He went to the doctor who could not find anything really wrong, so John made arrangements to go for a holiday in Corfu with four of his friends. What an ill-fated holiday that was! Two of his friends had to cancel, because their daughter was going into hospital for an operation. Then the other two cancelled, because the husband suffered a heart attack. All this worried John, but even though he felt so ill himself, he still intended going right until the night before flying, when he was visited by his niece Margaret. She insisted that he see his doctor again, as his condition had deteriorated to an alarming degree. Instead of going on holiday, he was rushed into hospital, where after blood tests leukaemia was diagnosed.

John spent many weeks in hospital, undergoing a severe kind of treatment. After a while our hearts were lightened, as he came home, and it seemed for a while that the disease was under control. Once a month he had to have a few days under treatment that was rather drastic. John used to say: "The first day is bad, the second day I wonder if it's worth it, the third day is even worse, but the fourth day I feel a bit better and after that I think it's all well worth while."

In between the treatments John worked hard for the Nottingham City Hospital's Leukaemia Research Fund. To raise money he made jams, pickles, lemon curd, and begged produce from his friends for a stall they had from time to time. He begged dozens of eggs from us, but he said they never reached the stall, as the nurses bought them as soon as they arrived at the hospital. No wonder! I used to pick out all the double-yolk ones. They were huge, and the nurses gave him one pound per dozen. He obtained over £200 for this fund, during that one last year of his life.

Poor John, he was feeling so well, when suddenly he went down with what we thought was a bout of influenza. Within a fortnight our much-loved brother died. The people of Wymeswold were shocked and shaken by the suddenness of his death. Donations to leukaemia research and to St. Mary's Church funds, requested instead of flowers, amounted to over £600, showing the great esteem people had for him.

Another deep sadness for my Wootton family around the same time as John's illness concerned our sister Lottie, who had been ailing for many years with Parkinson's disease. We had managed to keep her in her own home by organizing a rota of help from the rest of her family, including her nieces, especially her favourite niece Margaret, but one Sunday she collapsed and she has never walked again. The doctor told us we just had to agree now to allow her to be taken into hospital, as she would need day and night nursing. Being a dead weight and unable to help herself, she would have to be lifted, and we, her sisters, were all in our seventies and unable to do this. Lottie was admitted to St. Mary's Hospital in Melton Mowbray a few weeks before John died. We found it a big job visiting John in Nottingham fourteen miles north of Wymeswold and Lottie eleven and a half miles the other side of our village.

I feel that St. Mary's Hospital has become part of my life. I have learned such a lot about the sufferings of elderly women, who will live out their lives there or in a similar hospital, and about the kindness and wonderful patience of the sister and nurses of that ward. Whenever I take a friend to see Lottie, we divide our time between her and the others who like to talk to us.

At this time of writing there is a lady there who told me that seven years previously she had been decorating a ceiling, when she fell off the step-ladder. After a while she continued and finished the job, then she started to take her dog for a walk. "But," she said, "I did not get home, and here I have been all these years and never walked again." This lady is so good-looking, her hair is always in immaculate condition, and she wears her jewelry all the time. Her mind is so active, she reads a lot, and is immensely fond of music.

There is another lady, my favourite, who is paralysed from the neck down. I always think of her as one of nature's gentlewomen. She has the most beautiful expressive blue eyes I have ever seen in a lady over eighty years old.

One day my sister Florrie, who did not know the extent of this lady's illness, said to her: "I expect you read a lot." She answered: "My dear, I do not. I could not hold a book, or even turn over a page." This affected me greatly, and I just could not get it off my mind, when suddenly I thought: "She cannot read, but I could read to her."

On my next visit I asked permission to do just that, which was gladly given, for all the staff loved this delightful lady. When I asked her if she would like me to read to her my very first book, "Memories of a Country Girlhood", that David had had printed in Canada for my seventieth birthday, she was delighted, so one of the nurses brought Lottie in her chair to the side of the bed, then drew the curtains around us. I read two chapters every time I made a visit. They both appreciated my reading. Lottie had only read a few pages before coming to the hospital, and my friend said each time I left them: "Thank you, Nell, your reading is lovely, and such a change for me from looking at the ceiling all the time." It made me very happy to have finished the book before this very dear lady passed away. The staff and my family who all loved her were very sad at her passing.

A little before a trip I had arranged to make to Canada, Lottie suffered a serious relapse. On many occasions she seemed to be unconscious most of our

visiting time. When we spoke to her, she moved her lips but could not answer us. One day I asked her to nod her head, if she understood what I said, and shake her head if she could not. I asked her: "Do you know who is talking to you?" She nodded her head. Then I asked her a question to which the answer should be no, and she shook her head. By this method we were able to communicate with her to a small degree. This state of affairs went on and on. Three or four times, as we left her, we thought it might be the last time we should see her alive. I became increasingly worried about leaving her to go on my trip to Canada which was booked for the middle of August, but both my own family and my Wootton family insisted I must go. I felt torn two ways: I was aching to go to Canada, but I was deserting Lottie who might die while I was away.

At 8 a.m. on the morning before I was to leave, I received a telephone call from the hospital asking me to go there immediately, as Lottie was much worse and they thought I should be with her. I left everything in the hands of my friends the Jallands, and set off for Melton Mowbray. I stayed most of the day by Lottie's bed. I really thought she was dying: she could not speak and made no movement in answer to my questions. I thought: "How can I possibly leave her tomorrow?" But the hospital doctor decided for me. He took hold of both my arms and said: "You must go to Canada. I know your sister is very ill indeed, but you cannot do any more for her, and we will look after her." I knew this to be true: the care my sister had received from the sister and her staff was of the highest standard. When I said I felt like a deserter, he answered: "By all accounts you are no deserter, and I say you are to go." I thanked him and the staff for their care of my sister, and left the hospital with a heavy heart, believing I would never see her again. Next morning I rang the hospital to find that Lottie had rallied once again.

During this time Lottie was not my only worry: my youngest brother Bill had been rushed into Nottingham Hospital where they had done an emergency operation on his bowel. They said it was a bypass operation but they could not remove the growth, as it was inoperable. Our family was shattered. Bill had been the mainstay during all the sadness we had been called upon to bear. He and his wife Phyllis had looked after John right up to his death, with the help of their daughter Margaret. They had also been instrumental in enabling Lottie to stay in her own home much longer than would otherwise have been possible.

After I arrived home after visiting Lottie, I went to see Bill. He looked very poorly. But oh! how lucky he was to have Phyll for a wife, she is a born nurse, and he had two devoted daughters who were such a help to both of them. Both Bill and Phyll said I must certainly go to Canada, so I said goodbye, and the next day with a heavy heart I boarded my plane for Canada.

During my stay, which I shall write about in a later chapter, I phoned home a number of times: Bill was gaining strength, but Lottie remained the same, ebbing and flowing. On my return home I went over to see Lottie. She seemed unconscious and had suffered several bouts of a kind of fit. The nurses at that hospital were just marvellous, and with their devoted nursing, Lottie rallied once again, improving steadily week by week, but she did not regain the use of her legs. The doctor informed us that Lottie would never be able to live on her own again, so it looks as though she will have to spend the rest of her life in hospital.

Happily, brother Bill was told that, after a course of antibiotics, the inflammation had disappeared and the growth was now operable. After weeks of pain and discomfort Bill is now back to health and looks fine.

After Lottie had been in hospital for over a year, the family decided, with much sadness, that the house my parents had left to her to live in while she was able to manage it would have to be sold. It had been empty so long, it was gradually deteriorating. We were loath to start these proceedings until one day Lottie said to me: "Nell, the time has come when you will have to sell the house, and I want to tell you just what I want you to do about my home."

Lottie must have given this matter a lot of thought during her partial recovery. She told me exactly what she wanted us to do.

First, her brothers and sisters were to choose and take away whatever they liked. Second, her nephews and nieces were to do the same. She then gave me a list of her friends and neighbours in the order they were to go in and choose something they would like. After several articles had been sold, everything left was to be given to the Salvation Army.

This was a heavy load for me to manage, both mentally and physically, as most of the things in Lottie's home had belonged to our parents and these brought back many memories of our happy family life over many years. I was greatly helped by Bill's wife Phyll. I do not think I could have faced all this trauma without her help and encouragement. It was several weeks before we had the house cleared, because with my work on the poultry farm I could only manage a few hours each afternoon. Nearly every time I arrived home tired and trembling, after trying to control my emotion at seeing dismantled for ever the family home, where we had received such happiness and love from our parents. So I just sat down with a wee brandy until I recovered my equilibrium.

My Wootton family was delighted when Lottie's house was sold to a young couple with a family of several children.

During this time we were becoming increasingly worried about our brother Warner's health. Although he was eighty two years old, he had never had a serious illness during all those years of hard work in the building trade. Since the death of our parents, we had all thought of him as the head of the Wootton family. He was playing a game of indoor bowls when he was struck with dreadful pains and had to be brought home. The doctor was called and he suggested Warner must go into hospital for various tests. From that time Warner's health deteriorated so fast we knew that our brother, who had seemed so indestructible, was suffering with a terminal illness. I look back at the time when he was working on a roof near my own home, and he carried that long heavy ladder back to the builder's yard on his shoulder. Five weeks after that he died of cancer of the liver.

Our brothers Warner and John will be remembered for many years for their work in the village of Wymeswold, where one sees every few yards a house which they built or one they restored and modernised. They will also be remembered for the social work they helped with and enjoyed so much.

32

My First Book is Printed

I MUST now continue the story of how my stories, that I wrote exclusively for my grandchildren, came into print and sold over four thousand copies in just over two years without the aid of a professional publisher, but with the help and encouragement of the bookseller, W. H. Smith, as well as of many friends.

In the first place, my son David, a professor of French in the University of Toronto, picked up my scribble as I called it, read it and said: "Mother, this is very good. I think it would stand a fifty-fifty chance of being published." I smiled, because I thought: "Never in this world! Who would want to read stories of *my* youth apart from my own family?" My grandchildren loved to hear the same stories over and over again. They would creep into my bed, sometimes three of them at one time, all with the same request: "Please tell us a story, Grandma, about when you were a little girl." But never once, when I wrote them down, did I think of them as ever being published — that was, until the day of my seventy-fifth birthday.

I noticed on that particular morning that Susan had arrived for her work on the poultry-farm rather earlier than usual, but I passed no comment, as sometimes she did this to fit in with her home life. Then at exactly eleven o'clock, just as I was going to make our morning coffee, Sidney and Mary, along with their son Marcus, came in armed with two bottles of wine. Then most of my family living in Wymeswold trooped in. They all wished me a happy birthday, saying: "We must all drink to you, as this is a special birthday, seventy-five years old, three-quarters of a century." "Wait a minute," I said, "we must fetch in Susan and Ivor." But as I opened the door to fetch her, there she stood, with her usual lovely smile. Ivor came rushing up the drive on the tractor, as though all sorts of devils were after him. I can see him

now in my mind's eye, jumping off the tractor and sprinting to get here at the time they had all arranged. I made the remark: "You are all making a rare fuss of me on my seventy-fifth birthday."

As they all raised their glasses to wish me many happy returns, Sidney stepped forward and handed me a parcel. "Goodness!" I said, "another box of chocolates!" "No!" answered Sidney. "This is your life! And I have been dying to say that." I opened the parcel, and there were my stories of "Memories of a Country Girlhood" in a beautifully-bound hardback green book with gold lettering, and with a photo of me when I was twenty-one years old inside. I was so moved at the thought of my family having my memories privately printed, I just could not speak. To this day I cannot remember if I thanked them at the time, but how I wished that David could have been with us on that day, as it was he who had taken my manuscript home to Canada, edited it, typed it, and then had eight hardbacks and one hundred others duplicated for my birthday. David had been helped by

Susan, who illustrated the book, and by Gaynor, my granddaughter, who designed the title-page and the cover. That night we had a family party at that lovely hotel, Rothley Court, where Michael and Helen had held their wedding reception.

When I had recovered my composure sufficiently to talk clearly, I asked where all the other books were. I learned they were still in Canada, waiting for the next person to visit David to bring them home. Several of our friends and relations went that year, but they had rather a lot of luggage to carry, and I did not want them to pay excess baggage, so I was the one to go with a minimum of weight in one light suitcase, which enabled me to bring home the books.

David put them on the scales at Toronto airport. When I arrived at Birmingham airport, the minute the baggage-room door was opened, I ran to the first porter I could see with a pound note in my hand, and gasped out: "May I book you please?" "Course you can, me duck," he said. "Where's your luggage?" "I don't know," I answered, "we have to look for it." I said to him:

"You look for a large box — it is very heavy, I cannot even lift it — and I will search for my case." In those days at the old Birmingham airport the luggage was brought to a room in van-loads and placed around the inside walls where people could easily find it. I think this is much better than the modern way of the electric conveyor system, where the crowds waiting for their luggage often cannot get it until it has been round several times. We both soon found my case and the box, and the porter wheeled it out to the car, where Michael's Helen and her mother were waiting to take me home.

One of the first things I did after getting settled down at home again was to unpack the books. Then I wrote the names of all my grandchildren — yes, all fourteen of them — because it was written especially for them, then I started with all my nephews and nieces. Each of them was sent a copy. David had already posted one to each of my brothers and sisters. After sending these, I had around fifteen left, so those who had asked if they could buy one were given one and I wrote their names inside. They insisted they pay, but I told them I could not charge for them, when I had been given them for my birthday. When they insisted, I suggested they donate to cancer research and to church funds. A number of those friends donated much more than the book cost, but they said they had enjoyed it so much.

The good reception these hundred copies enjoyed encouraged me to see about publishing "Memories" in larger numbers. I enquired around a little and, when David came home for a summer visit, we got into the car and sounded out a couple of printers. The cost of resetting the book was too high, so we decided to duplicate the original but reduce its format from 8 × 11 inches to the size of this book, and to bring it out in paperback. David thought I should order 500 or at the most 1,000 copies. We discussed paper quality, sewing of the spine and other questions of presentation, then asked for an estimate. We settled on AB Printers of Leicester.

I remember well a later visit to this printer to make the decisions concerning the book. It was on 11 August 1983. Susan Jalland and I had worked very hard all morning to get our work on the poultry-farm finished in time to keep our appointment. I locked up my house and was getting into my car when I thought I would just have a walk round my poultry-houses, just to make sure everything was alright, because I disliked leaving the place unattended during extremely hot weather. Lizbeth had gone to Melton Mowbray with the children to visit Lottie in hospital and Ivor had taken a load of eggs into Nottingham market.

What a good job I took this look around! I had only gone a few yards when I smelled burning. I quickened my pace, almost running round each poultry-house until in one of them I found one of the huge fans burning itself out. I was amazed at this happening, because that particular fan had been installed only a few weeks previously at a cost of over £80. I hastily switched off at the main supply, then tried to get in touch with our electrician but failed to locate him. I rang the firm which rewinds our fans, and they promised to send a man out during the afternoon.

What worried me was the fact that, if fans cease to function in hot weather, the birds suffer dreadfully, and sometimes great losses can occur through lack of oxygen. I have been very fortunate in having Mr. Fred James, our electrician, who will leave any work to attend to this kind of emergency. We also have a generator of our own to use in case of power cuts, and this has prevented any catastrophe happening in hot weather, and has certainly saved a major drop in egg production. Our bungalow and Michael's house and buildings also benefit from this generator when power cuts occur. It enables us to carry on normally, even boiling a kettle of water for neighbours during a lengthy power failure.

To get back to our appointment with the printer which was for between 2 and 3 p.m., we made it, but only just, and there, much to my surprise, for the time being at least, I ceased to worry about my birds. Susan and I, being such complete novices at setting about publishing a book, were completely enthralled by what we learned. We discovered that, when a book is published, it has to have an ISBN number, and six copies have to be sent to London under the terms of the Copyright Act of 1911. These are sent to each of the following: the British Library, the libraries of the Universities of Oxford and Cambridge, the National Library of Scotland, the Library of Trinity College, Dublin, and the National Library of Wales.

How glad I was to have Susan with me to help make some of the decisions, like the size of the book, the quality of the paper, the kind of cover, the colours for the cover (we chose blue and white), and lastly the number to order. The printer, like David, was very cautious: both thought 1,000 copies would take a lot of selling. Susan and I were more optimistic because, prior to seeing the printer, I had taken one of the books David had produced in Canada to W. H. Smith's of Loughborough, asking their advice as regards selling it in their shop. After they had read it, they told me to "get cracking", as they were sure it would sell well. I had also received permission to sell it on my market-stall. Having around 800 customers, many of whom knew I had written a book, and wanted to read it, I felt I could sell well over 1,000 copies. Susan and I had talked the number over together, and it was Susan who finally said: "Let's have 2,000." Rightly, as it turned out, we took the plunge.

These books were being paid for by money left to me by my much-loved brother John, who had recently died of leukaemia. I decided to donate to leukaemia research 20p of the price of each book we sold privately and to dedicate the book to him.

Susan and I came home from the printers in a very happy frame of mind, thinking what a lot we had learned about publishing a book. Unfortunately, we found that the electrician had not been. The temperature in that house had risen to between eighty and ninety degrees. The birds were beginning to look distressed: they stood with their wings down and their beaks wide open. We made ourselves a cup of tea, and while we were drinking it, the electrician arrived to take out the fan for rewiring. Then our own electrician came with a loose fan borrowed from another farmer which blew cool air into the house, clearing it in a very short time.

The next day, which was not quite so hot, another trouble with the electricity caused the cleaning-out system to break down, and that job had to be all done by hand. "Let's hope for a better day on the farm tomorrow," we said. In spite of these problems Susan and I went to bed thrilled with our meeting with the printers.

33

Publication and Reception
of "Memories"

ON October 26th 1983, when I was 75 years old, I stood and watched with great delight as 2,050 copies of my first book, "Memories of a Country Girlhood", were delivered at my home in Wymeswold. After they were stacked in a corner of my spare bedroom, I stood and gazed at that huge pile of books and thought: "Good gracious me! Will we ever sell that lot?" But yes, we did. With the help of my many good friends, splendid reviews of the book in our local papers, a chat on Radio Leicester and Radio Nottingham, we sold all of the 2,050 copies, and at this time of writing over 600 of a reprint of 1,150 copies have already been sold. W. H. Smith's of Loughborough, Leicester, Melton Mowbray and Nottingham, along with a number of small bookshops in

Leicestershire, sold many copies. Shops and pubs in Wymeswold have also sold a large number, giving the discount to their own special charity, but most of them swelled the amount to my special charity, Leukaemia Research. By the end of 1983, £145 had been donated to the Queen's Medical Centre in Nottingham. During those eight weeks before Christmas I seemed to be living in a state of happy shock. I wrote "Memories of a Country Girlhood" without a thought that my stories would ever be published. This enterprise has altered my whole life, bringing me many friends, and contacts with people who have bought the book for both county and university libraries. Even historians have written to me who are interested in how we lived in English villages during and since the early 1900s. I had no idea I was writing a history of village life until the proprietor of a bookshop in Toronto, who was going to sell my book, told me it had more reality than another very expensive book he was selling. I am also very happy to have received large orders outside of Leicestershire like one from Derbyshire

County Library which bought around fifty copies. Several of the librarians have told me they have a long waiting-list of readers, and that as soon as the books are returned, they are taken out again.

Here are some of the reactions to my book. They are included here because they brought me pleasure and I hope they will not bore my readers. Some people reading this book will recognize what they themselves have said. Some of the remarks which I treasure were made during the first few weeks after publication. A friend said: "Thank you, Nell, for a lovely book. I shall treasure it all my life, for it was written with love, and it shows." My daughter Lizbeth said: "Wouldn't it make a nice television serial." Many people said the same thing, only adding: "After all the blood and thunder and misery seen on our screens, that book would make an interesting and happy change."

I left one book at a farmer's place, where they had suffered atrocious luck during the year 1983. The farmer had been accident-prone, having had three accidents one after the other. The last one had been the worst and had incapacitated him completely. To add insult to injury, a spark from a tractor had set his dutch barn on fire, destroying both the barn and its contents. His wife told me he had become very depressed, but my book had been as good as a doctor's tonic to him, for not only did it make him smile, he was really chuckling over it. Then she bought seven more books for Christmas presents. I was overcome with delight, not just for the sale of seven more books, but with the thought that my stories had lifted her husband out of his depression, if only for a short time.

A lady customer at my stall said: "Ellen, I bought your book 'Memories of a Country Girlhood', and immediately afterwards took to my bed with bronchitis, where I read it with such delight I wished very much your second book had been published." Then she added: "When will that be, Ellen?" I answered: "When I have sold 1,500 of number one, I will be able to afford to have number two printed."

Another customer said: "All our family are reading your book, Ellen, but we have only reached half way, because, you see, we all go to work, and the one who arrives home first commandeers it, so not one of us has been able to finish it."

The next lady really entertained us. In her droll kind of voice, she described passages where she said she had lived through every word. She entertained our other customers by telling them about a journey my friend Flo Tyler and I suffered in a bad blizzard, coming home from Loughborough one dark night. "Ooeer!" she explained. "As I read about that journey I lived every inch of the way with you." By the time she had finished relating all this, the queue around my egg-stall had grown and grown, but I must add that her performance sold quite a number of books.

During that first fortnight many customers told me they had sent one abroad for a Christmas present. America, Canada, Australia, New Zealand and Spain were the countries most mentioned. South Africa and Germany have since been added.

A neighbouring stall-holder bought one the first week. The following week she bought several more for Christmas presents, with the remark: "I loved your book, Mrs. Smith, but I must admit to feeling just a little bit jealous, not because you have written such a lovely book, but because of your wonderfully happy childhood, living with such a happy family." A very special customer sent a book to a friend in Canada, who read it to old people living in a home called Versa Care. To her delight several of these old people became excited, because as the story unfolded, they recognized places, and likened some of the stories to what had happened to them in their youth. When the reading ended, they begged the lady, whose name I now know to be Ivy Johnson, to let the author know how very much they had enjoyed the book. I was certainly overjoyed to know that my simple stories had given pleasure to so many old people living in Canada.

A lady who was a complete stranger to me came to the stall and asked if I was the lady who had written "Memories of a Country Girlhood". When I answered "Yes", she said: "Thank you very much. That book made my Christmas." Then she walked away.

On another occasion a young couple, both strangers to me, called at the stall to tell me that they had taken a copy to a very old friend one evening after they had finished work. The next morning, before going to work, they received a phone call from their friend saying how she loved the book. When they said: "How do you know, as you can't have read it all yet?" she answered: "Oh yes I have. I took it to bed with me and I just could not go to sleep with a book like that in my hand. I lived my life all over again."

As a contrast in age groups, within 15 minutes of this couple's visit, a young woman asked for a book, saying: "I have bought one before, which all members of the family have read, but my eleven-year old daughter has begged for one she can call her very own." A book which was sent to New Zealand was enjoyed by a family that had lived in Wymeswold for two years then emigrated. One of the remarks sent to their English friends was: "Thank you very much, you could not have sent us anything nicer, even if you could have sent us the moon."

34

My Third Holiday in Canada

ON May 22nd 1984 I left to spend a holiday in Canada with my son David and his family. I was lucky on this trip, travelling on the plane with a couple from Leicester who were so pleasant they made the journey seem much shorter. I travelled from Birmingham to Toronto with Wardair, a Canadian airline which really looks after its passengers. A young stewardess carried my holdall right on to the plane. We had the choice of many kinds of wine and spirits, and as many as one liked at no extra cost. I rarely drink any intoxicants during the day — just a sherry or a wee brandy, when I get into bed, to help encourage sleep — but on that plane I drank two glasses of wine with my dinner and two brandies afterwards, which certainly had the desired effect of sending me to sleep for several hours.

David had asked me to take over to Canada sixty copies of my book "Memories of a Country Girlhood". Oh dear! they were so heavy, I could not even lift my case, let alone carry it, so I was hoping I would be able to obtain help on reaching Toronto. Michael had taken me to Birmingham airport and had carried the case right up to the scales, but I was unlucky at Toronto. Two men helped by lifting it off the electric conveyor, then I stood third place in a small queue waiting my turn for one of the three porters to carry my case to the gate, where David was waiting. To my surprise and disgust, each one pushed me gently to one side and passed me by, so they could take a family's luggage of three cases, and even five cases, for which they would expect a much larger tip than from one old lady with just one case. Now what could I do with a case I could not lift? So I dragged it to one side out of people's way, and searched for an inspector whom I found standing near the gate, where all the people were waiting to meet their friends. As I started to tell him of my difficulty, David called out "Mother" from the other side of the gate. The inspector asked: "Is that your son?" When I said "Yes", he called David to come in to carry my case. I breathed a sigh of relief, as I watched David walk towards me, and in a matter of minutes we were settled in David's car and on our fourteen-mile journey to his house.

The first few days the weather was lovely, but for the next fortnight it was so hot and humid it made us try to find the coolest possible spot, which was the basement of their house. At night it was so hot one's hair was wet moments after touching the pillow.

In a matter of one week David had edited my second book. The question was: what was to be its title? All the time I was writing the manuscript, I was searching in my mind for a suitable title, but had made no definite decision. One evening David said very quietly: "I have a title for your second book, Mother." When I asked: "What is that, David?", he answered: "Seven Pennies in My Hand". That was it, no more wondering as to its title, "Seven Pennies in My Hand" it was.

To some people it might seem a funny title for a book mostly about farming and country life, but one chapter contains a delightful story about my two small sons who asked me to close my eyes and hold out my hand, into which they placed all their pocket money, seven pennies between them. They said these were to help buy their mummy a new fur coat. I was extremely touched by this gift, and many people who have read the book have told me they had a good cry when reading this section. One ten-year-old girl said to her mother: "I can't help it, Mummy, but I cry every time I read that chapter!"

I had been very surprised when David had written asking me, when I went to Canada, to take sixty copies of "Memories of a Country Girlhood" with me, but to know all is to understand all. The understanding came when a lady named Ivy Johnson invited us over to her home in Brantford, over 100 miles from Toronto. A friend of hers who was one of my egg customers, had sent her the book for a Christmas present. She had liked it so much, she would not even lend it to her own sister, in case it got lost, until she was sure that she could buy another one. Her English friend had told her I had a son in Toronto named David, and that he was working in the French department at the University of Toronto. Ivy had got in touch with David to find out if she could buy more copies of the book. When he had told her I was visiting Toronto the following May, and that he was quite sure I would take some over, she had offered to be my agent to sell my book, and had made a date when we should take them over to Brantford.

When David said we were to be there by 9:30 a.m., I thought it a bit early to be invited to a complete stranger's home. We were only a few miles from our destination when David dropped the bombshell. Ivy Johnson had arranged for the three of us to be on Brantford radio at 11 a.m. I was a bit shaken but pleased my book was worthy of a talk-in on radio about it. Ivy's husband, Len, had drawn a map to make it easy to find their house and David got there without any trouble.

Ivy and Len were sitting out on their lawn waiting to greet us with such a warmth of welcome we felt immediately at home.

This completely happy day went like this. First, we had a chat together over a cup of coffee. Then we went on to Versa Care, where Ivy worked as the Activity Officer. Versa Care is the most beautiful home for the elderly I have ever seen, and is well worth describing in this book. The story started with a vicar, the Reverend Peterson, losing his voice fifteen years ago. Unable to continue in the ministry, he bought a large house, and along with his wife started a nursing-home for the elderly. From that small beginning the beautiful home called Versa Care was built, accommodating between three and four hundred old people and covering many acres of beautifully-kept grounds. The home had a hospital wing for the very ill, which we did not see. The first part we entered was a large room with a shop down one side, where many articles were made and sold by the residents. In this room Ivy had arranged to have my photograph taken, along with the vicar and a married couple living in the home. The photographer was late arriving, so we had to leave without it being taken, or we would have been late at Radio Brantford. We all enjoyed our half-hour's chat, and the interviewer said she hoped she would see us again the next time I visited Canada. A kind thought of Len, whom we left at home, was a gift to me of a tape of our radio talk. Each time I hear it I live that happy day all over again, listening to David and Ivy's voices.

After the radio chat it was back to Versa Care, where we were given a splendid lunch. Then the photographer arrived, so we found the vicar and the old couple, and we were placed together, with me in the middle holding up one of my books. This turned out to be a very good photo of each of us and another thing I value about that day. Ivy then showed us around part of this huge complex, starting with the entertainment room which had a stage at one end. Then we went to look at some of the residents' rooms, some of which were occupied by married couples using their own furniture, others were for single people. All the rooms were beautifully kept and highly polished, and these old people were absolutely delighted to show us them. Then we all made our way to a communal room with a kitchen unit at one end where they could make tea. There I was asked to give a talk about my No. 1 book, but I suggested a talk about No. 2 book, as Ivy had read No. 1 to them. They loved it, and asked many questions.

I was very moved when a tiny old lady presented me with a beautiful spray of artificial flowers, in a plastic holder full of sweets. I noticed this bouquet was made in Holland. We then went back to the restaurant for tea, where a lady reporter was waiting to interview us for an article in her paper, the Brantford Expositor.

Ivy told us she had prepared everything in readiness for a dinner at her home, but David told her she had worked hard that day to give us pleasure, that her prepared dinner would do for the next day, and that he was taking us all out for a steak that night. Those last few hours chatting over our meal were a delight. We said

416

our goodbyes thinking we had made two wonderful new friends, and then started the 100-odd miles back home to Toronto.

Ivy sold many of my books among her friends in Canada, one of whom came to see me when he and his wife visited London.

35

Travelling in Canada

I SPENT three weeks in Canada with David and his family. We travelled more than usual, so as soon as I had time, I wrote down where we had been and some of the things we had done. As a result I can read my account years afterwards and live it over again.

After about a week at home, we started our travels by going north through Ontario and into Quebec. Our first stop was at Young's Point, where David and his daughter Catherine hired a canoe. While getting into it, David managed to tip it over. He got wet and his camera fell into the water. He dried it out, but it did not work, so he took it to a shop that repaired cameras. But they told him it was a write-off, as it would cost more to put right than the cost of a new one. David thanked them politely and took it to the next shop he saw. In all, four people told him the same story, so David started fiddling about with it himself, and was successful in making it work and he still uses it without benefit of the light metre.

We stayed at an old inn that first night, where David asked if they had a spin dryer. They had not, so he took his wet clothes to a laundrette at a caravan site, where he did the job quite satisfactorily. The inn was a poor set-up. Apparently the owner had sold it, but the new owners had not been able to keep up the mortgage payments, so he had fore-closed on them and taken it over again. Several things had been taken away, even the piano, which had been replaced with an old worn-out one. The proprietor was trying to run the place with his wife and one maid, but not very successfully, while looking for another buyer. The beds were alright, but the food was poor. That day we saw the boats being let through the locks, which was very interesting.

Our next stop was Peterborough, to look at the university which my granddaughter Ingrid thought she might like as her first choice. Not one of us liked it. We thought it a sombre-looking place, more like a prison than a university, although it might have been alright inside. A further few miles and we called and looked at Lakefield College where Prince Andrew spent part of his educational life. We then drove on to a ferry-boat which took us over the Ottawa River to Quyon, Quebec.

We stayed in Ottawa two nights in a skyscraper hotel. Our room was on the twenty-second floor. When we looked down through the windows, the cars looked little larger than match-boxes. We left Catherine with friends in Ottawa. Less than half a mile from where her friends lived, we halted at some lights. We already knew something serious had happened, because we had been stopped several times by armed police at certain points, and police cars had passed us at a terrific speed. David said: "I think someone has been killed." Just the other side of the lights a man lay sprawled across his steering-wheel. We learned from the car wireless a few moments later that it was the military attaché to the Turkish Embassy that had been assassinated. Armenians were suspected, but they got away and were not captured while I was in Canada. Police said it was the first time a diplomat had been killed in Ottawa. No country seems immune from these terrible killings.

We left Ottawa quite early. Our first stop was to visit the Château Montebello, where the heads of state of many nations, including our own Margaret Thatcher, had met that year. This hotel, set in the most beautiful grounds, was built entirely of logs, both inside and out. The inside logs were highly polished, but electric lights had to be used all the time, otherwise it would have been extremely dark. Olaug said: "I would love to have a meal here, just to be able to say 'I dined at the Château Montebello.'" Unfortunately, their prices were very expensive, more than we felt justified in spending for a midday meal, but that restaurant seen from the top of the stairway was something to remember. We strolled around the hotel and eventually found a basement cafeteria that catered to people like us. There we had many choices of dishes, so Olaug was able to say after all: "Yes, we dined at the Château Montebello."

We travelled in a ferry-boat a second time which saved many miles of motoring. That night we stayed at a lovely hotel called the Pension Wunderbar (pronounced vunderbar) at Wakefield in the Gatineau Hills. The proprietors, who were Austrian, asked us to take off our shoes before entering, putting them in trays provided. Not content with asking us, they had posted printed notices ordering us to take off our shoes. They told us they did not usually take visitors on chance, only those who were recommended, but for once they would, to oblige us. We only saw one other visitor, so perhaps they needed us rather badly.

After Wakefield we went to see the house of a former Canadian Prime Minister, Mackenzie King, before continuing on our journey towards the Thousand Islands, which are situated at the eastern end of Lake Ontario, where it becomes the St. Lawrence River. We obtained our tickets for a one and a half hour cruise around the Thousand Islands. We started in daylight and ended the cruise facing the sunset. There are around 1,800 islands, many of them with beautiful houses built by rich men from both America and Canada. A castle was started on Heart Island by a man named Boldt for his wife, but unfortunately she died before the castle was finished, so the work was stopped. We passed a large island and a small one with only a few yards of water between them which was spanned by the smallest bridge only thirty-two feet long. This is the smallest international bridge in the world. The small island is on American territory, and the large one on Canadian. Most of these beautiful islands are named after either a British admiral or battleship. Children who live on these islands use boats in the summer to go to school, and in winter they skate over the ice. Huge ships of all nations use this inland seaway, but in winter it freezes solid and sometimes it has been known to trap ships in the ice. This was a very impressive trip that I shall remember all my life.

Before we left the town of Gananoque,

we had a splendid dinner, but unfortunately Catherine left her handbag in the restaurant and did not realize it until she got out of the car, as she slept nearly all the way home. Olaug was the only one who remembered the name of the place. The next morning she rang to enquire if they had found it. They had, so Olaug posted off a cheque to cover the postage, and five dollars for their trouble. Instead of a returned handbag, a returned cheque arrived with an apology, saying they had put the handbag underneath the pay-desk, and it had been stolen. The lady was very upset.

Catherine is a dab hand at leaving her handbags in restaurants. I remember that, when I went on holiday with them to Devon, we came back by way of Bath, and there, too, Catherine left her handbag. Once again Olaug remembered the name of the restaurant, David rang, found they still had her handbag, and asked if they would save it until called for. Fortunately Sidney and Mary were going to Bath for a cousin's wedding the next week-end, so it ended happily for Catherine that time.

Once when I was in Canada we all went on a bus, and Catherine left her purse on the seat. I saw it and picked it up, sliding it into my pocket, hoping she would suddenly remember she had left it. I had surreptitiously shown it to Olaug, who after a while kept throwing out sly hints, such as: "Have we got everything?" "Oh dear!" moaned Catherine, "I have lost my purse." We allowed her to suffer for about fifteen minutes, after which I slipped the purse into her hand. She shouted joyfully: "Thank you, Grandma" over and over again. Then she hugged me in the middle of the pavement or, as the Canadians say, the sidewalk.

On one of the last few days of my stay in Canada David took me and my grandchild Gaynor and her boyfriend, who were also staying with David, to see a winery. It was fascinating to see all those huge vats or barrels holding thousands of gallons of wine in each of them. The cleanliness was first-class: the wood barrels and brass bands around them were polished to a high degree. On entering the building, everyone was given a glass of wine, and before leaving we all

sat down to a wine-tasting session. They had twelve bottles of different kinds of wine and champagne. They poured out half a glass of the wine of your choice, after which you were given a biscuit with a tiny bit of cheese. Then you started all over again, half a glass of wine, then biscuit and cheese. The party next to us tasted nearly every one until they were quite merry. I tasted only two and felt a bit light-headed. I bought several bottles of wine for David's dinner parties, but I did not see the hard-drinking party next to us buy any.

We then travelled to Niagara-on-the-Lake to see "The Desert Song". I wondered how they could act that on a small stage, but it was really good and we enjoyed it immensely. Gaynor and her friend went off on their own, and we met them at the car around midnight, but before starting for home we called to see Niagara Falls floodlit. What a spectacular sight the falls are, and the noise is deafening! Then we started our ninety-mile journey home, arriving there about two in the morning.

36

Farms for Sale

IN a period of less than two years my eldest and youngest sons each became the new owners of farms, Sidney moving over 100 miles to the south-west and Richard establishing himself about the same distance to the north of our native village.

When Sidney's second son, Marcus, finished his three years at Cirencester Agricultural College, he married a Welsh girl and started working on his father's farm. They realized that, for the two of them, they needed more land and, as land seldom came up for sale in the village, they decided to sell the Wymeswold farm and buy another, preferably somewhere closer to North Wales, from where Marcus's wife hails.

To my dismay the Wymeswold land was sold before they had another farm in view. Fortunately, after months of searching, Sidney, Mary, Marcus and Ann found their dream farm near Bromyard, in Herefordshire. They bought it and moved in on July 29th, 1982.

One just cannot imagine the enormous amount of work this move entailed. Moving house is daunting, and they had more than one furniture-van load, taking two days. Then there were the implements, large and small, like tractors and trailers and that great combine harvester, all travelling around 100 miles on very busy roads. Even the cats, which always lived outside, had to be rounded up and taken to the new farm. Somehow, when these terrific jobs need facing, strength and staying power seem to be given.

I shall never forget the first time I saw their beautiful manor house (which incidentally has a conservation order on it). To the right on entering the drive is a huge shrubbery. For Mary, who is a flower arranger, it is paradise. On the left is a tennis court, but it looks as though it has not been used for a long time. Seen from the front, the house is a three-storey Georgian building. It forms the top of a letter T, the tail of which is the older original house, built in stone. Sidney and Mary live in the front part, Marcus and Ann have made the back part their home after a lot of restoring has been done. This took a long time as they had to obtain permission of the council and the conservation people. Counting the huge cellars and bathrooms, there are thirty rooms all told. The entrance hall and the two upstairs landings are the size of a good-sized room. The imposing staircase in a beautifully polished wood has no stair carpet, as it would be a shame to cover up such beauty.

The view from the front of this house is breathtakingly lovely. Stepping out of the front door, one crosses the drive, on to a grass terrace, then on through a gate into a parkland of around twenty acres with many majestic trees, one of which is a cedar whose shape and size are spectacular. At the bottom end of the park is a trout lake. All the land, amounting to around 175 acres, surrounds this beautiful manor house, park and lake. The day I first saw all this was beautiful, the sun was shining, and as we stood in front of the house, we had an exceptionally clear view for miles over the Malvern Hills, one of the most beautiful places in England. As we all stood there, I remember just what I said to Sidney and Mary: "I never thought a child of mine would ever own and live in such a mansion, set in these beautiful surroundings."

After settling into their new farm, Sidney sold his Wymeswold farm-house, the garden and orchard, along with all the farm buildings and dutch barns. Houses have now been built there. Now only two of my children live in Wymeswold, Michael in the family farm at Wysall Lane End and Lizbeth living next door to me. I am indeed lucky to have them so near but I do miss Sidney and his family very much. I stop myself fretting by working hard on my poultry farm in the day time and by writing in the evenings, knowing full well they are wonderfully happy and contented in their new farm, and that Sidney's ambition of obtaining that kind of place has been fulfilled.

Richard became a farmer for the first time at the age of almost forty. Around

Christmas 1983 he became one of the army of the unemployed. After three months without a job, when his redundancy money was in danger of being used for normal living, he saw a poultry-farm advertised in north-west Yorkshire. After several anxious weeks of negotiations he bought the farm, which has eight and a half acres of land, with poultry-houses for 20,000 laying hens and two rearing-houses. The farm is well equipped with everything needed to carry on a business which sells the majority of its eggs to shops. Two good vans, one of which is nearly new, tractors and trailers, and two slurry-tanks which get rid of the manure to farmers living in the neighbourhood, are also included. There are two huge store-houses, one used for packaging and storing eggs, the other for housing the tractors, vans and car. Down one side of the latter there is a long work-bench with many tools. The room for grading and storing eggs had been converted from an old barn, adjoining the farm-house. The stone-built farmhouse has five bedrooms, a beautiful kitchen with light-oak built-in units, a small dining room, and a sitting room.

Apart from the kitchen every room needed redecorating, not because they were in bad shape, but the colours were not Richard's and Eirene's idea of decoration. The staircase and landing were bright orange. One large bedroom was in two shades of royal blue, and another bedroom was decorated in bright pillar-box red. So much redecorating would take a great deal of time, and on a farm with over 20,000 birds time for other work was in very short supply. Fortunately, Richard and Eirene had a very good friend named Derek who was an experienced decorator. He came most week-ends and worked hard to hasten the completion of this work. First the staircase and landing were painted white, and a lovely blue carpet covered the stairs and landing. Then Eirene fixed a few good pictures and blue and white antique plates on the walls. An old oak chest with blue china on the top and a lovely little antique sofa along one wall completed this charming miniature gallery. On my second visit one bedroom was finished, and another nearly so. Eirene finished the paintwork during my few days with them, so only the furniture needed placing after I left. The next room to tackle is the bright red room. I expect the next time I visit them that will have been stripped and papered. The elder children help strip their own rooms, and Ricky chose the paper and colours of his very large room, and did most of the decorating himself.

On one of my visits with them I became the owner of a jet black dog, a cross between a whippet and a labrador. It happened like this. On one of her rounds Eirene was delivering eggs to a farm where she saw this one and a half-year-old bitch, heavy in pup, and so thin every rib showed. Eirene, who has a great love for dogs, was very concerned at the dog's condition and remonstrated with the farmer for allowing it to become such a pitiful object. She told him she had a good mind to take it away from him, and he answered: "Take the bugger, she ain't any good. But she's 'ad to look after 'ersen apart from a few cracked eggs and a drop of milk." Eirene took her home, and that night she had seven puppies which were all black.

Now Eirene had the job of finding homes for them. Two were sold for £5 each, two went to the R.S.P.C.A., and the children kept two, which left one puppy and the mother to find homes for. After a lot of persuasion our Michael took to the puppy and brought it home to Wymeswold, much to his wife's displeasure, as they had enough dogs on the farm without another puppy, but it was not long before Brian their son caught her making a fuss of the puppy. Brian exclaimed: "Mother, what are you doing?" "Oh, nothing," answered Helen, not liking to be caught fondling the puppy she did not want.

With all the puppies gone, this left only the mother needing a home. Since the loss of my husband I had always said I would never have another dog, but during that day this dog stole my heart. She kept coming up to me, laying her head gently on my knee, and looking up at me with such beautiful and expressive eyes, I just could not resist her. So with the children pleading and Eirene saying: "Grandma, she is very well behaved and has only one fault, she wanders off a bit" — a remark I later remembered with sorrow — I brought the dog home. After a few weeks, when her milk had gone, I took her to the vet and had all the injections necessary for her future health. Then she had the operation to save having more puppies.

After I had enjoyed several months of delight in the devotion she gave me, she wandered on to the road and was killed instantly by a passing car. A young man knocked urgently on my door one Saturday afternoon, asking me if I owned a black labrador dog. I answered: "No, but my daughter next door owns one." He raced away, and I followed with dread in my heart, hoping nothing had happened to their labrador, Sammy. The young man said his car had killed a jet black labrador, and a lady on the road had told him it belonged to the people up the lane. The young man was greatly upset, saying Lizbeth must not see the dog, as it was not a pretty sight. Lizbeth started to cry saying: "How ever am I going to tell the children?" As she went into another room to control herself, their dog Sammy sauntered up the drive. I called to Lizbeth: "It is not Sammy, he is here." Then I knew it was my dog Sheba. That young man picked up a spade and did the necessary work in clearing up the tragedy of my lovable dog.

I miss her in so many ways. When I was working in my garden, she would creep up to me, tucking her head under my arm in such a loving kind of way. She was so obedient. I had taught her not to go on the flower-garden, to come immediately on call, but the one thing I had not managed to cure was the occasional walk down the drive and on to the road. I expect this wandering was inherent in her, caused by fending for herself during her early life with the Yorkshire farmer. I do not think I will ever have another dog, but oh! how I miss her enthusiastic welcome, when I drive home. After I had been a short while away, she nearly went mad with excitement when she heard my car coming up the drive.

37

My Grandchildren

MY two eldest grandchildren married recently, first Marcus, Sidney's second son, then his first-born, Kevin, whose new daughter Eleanor is my first and only great-grandchild.

When Marcus married Jean Ann Walker on September 20th, 1980, the guests from Wymeswold had to travel many miles to Llangollen in North Wales. The ladies discussed what they were going to wear, and all but myself decided they were going to have a new rig-out. I decided that my last new outfit had only been worn a few times, I liked it very much, and was quite sure it would do quite well. This was a very unpopular decision with my female relatives. Mary, Marcus's mother, said: "You really must have a new outfit, Mother, for the first wedding of one of your grandsons."

Kathleen, my sister-in-law, bless her, tried her very best to persuade me to lash out on a really good-class rig-out. I still insisted I did not really need one, until one day when I was in Nottingham, I saw a length of rusty-red material hanging from the ceiling to the floor. Without hesitation I bought a length of this lovely material, but an imp of mischief prompted me to keep it a secret from everyone but my friend Susan Jalland who would help me with the fittings. I decided to make a dress with a cape, which when finished looked really classy. According to Susan, I had an outfit that in a shop would have cost at least £70. With making it myself, it cost only £7. Mary and Kathleen were so pleased when they saw the new outfit at the wedding, although it was a bit startling for a woman in her seventies to wear such a bright colour. "Mutton dressed as lamb" as the saying goes. But there, I enjoyed wearing it!

It was a beautiful wedding. Ann, who is a tiny person, looked beautiful in white, and Gaynor, the only bridesmaid, who was dressed in a shell-pink dress, looked quite regal. The service was held in the village church of Llangollen. The flowers were breathtakingly lovely. The reception was held at the Bryn Howel Hotel. After the meal and speeches the room was cleared for dancing. I found myself for the first time since Sid's death really enjoying dancing once again. Having David and Olaug home from Canada for the wedding was an extra special joy to all, even though Olaug had to leave after the meal to catch her plane home to Canada. Marcus and Ann bought a house in the next village of Burton-on-the-Wolds where they lived until they moved to Bromyard.

When my eldest grandson married Diana Reed down in the county of Cornwall, it seemed a special occasion, for several families and friends of Kevin arranged to spend a few days holiday, staying at the Poldark Inn, in Delabole. They were married at St. Minver Church, on October 8th, 1983. Diana looked regal in a white dress, and her bridesmaid was dressed in pink taffeta. The church had been decorated by lady members of the church, who must have been professionals at flower arranging, their work was so splendid. Although a terrific wind greeted us as we emerged from the church, numerous fine photos were taken. The reception was held at the Poldark Inn, with around eighty guests. After the reception the guests were invited to join in the dance that was taking place later in the evening. We were lucky as it was a special old-time dance, which most of the guests enjoyed.

Diana and Kevin were making their home in Manchester in the house that Kevin had bought when he obtained a new job in that city. The following July they had a baby girl, whom they named Eleanor. This baby made me a great-grandmother for the first time, and my brothers and sisters, my sister-in-law and my brother-in-law, great-great-aunties and uncles. This baby certainly makes one realize one's age, even if one does not feel it, but there, as the old saying goes: "One is as old as one feels." How true that is! I am one of the lucky ones — 79 years old, and still going strong, working with my poultry and writing quite a bit.

Since I lost Sid, I love more than ever having my grandchildren to stay with me. Their love and devotion to me over the years have grown, not diminished. This has so often lifted me out of loneliness and despair, especially in those early years of my loss. They will work hard for me as well as play.

I remember one year David and his family spent most of their summer holiday with me. Ingrid, the older of the two girls, decided to spend a day in Nottingham with her mother and her Auntie Lizbeth. Catherine wanted to stay home with me and her cousins who were also staying on the farm. We decided to tidy up the whole poultry-farm. All joined in. Anything lying around was picked up with the words: "Is this any good? Can this be burned, Grandma?" By the time we were ready to light this huge bonfire, the children were filthy, but my! didn't they enjoy that fire! Each time it burned low, the children worked frantically to find more refuse. At the finish they were even bringing in barrowloads of dry potato tops from all over the field. At last, black as ink and unutterably weary, the children staggered into the house for a nice warm bath, and after a nice little rest ate an enormous tea.

When Ingrid arrived home from Nottingham and Catherine told her of the wonderful time she and her cousins had had with the bonfire, she was furious, because she had missed all the fun. She pleaded with me to light another one, and child-like, not realizing we could not find rubbish for another one, threw a tantrum, hoping I could miraculously make some appear for her benefit. Ingrid was a long time getting over this disappointment.

Since I have had a full set of false teeth, each grandchild, from the time they could only just talk, used to ask me to take out my teeth. Then I would say: "I will take mine out, if you will take yours out." They would try and try, but could not understand why I could and they could not. They love it when I take out my teeth, take off my glasses, put my hair behind my ears and pull funny faces, but best of all these young ones love to creep into my bed each morning for the stories I tell.

When Richard and Eirene with their

five children came, we were a right good houseful, but it always made me glad we had three bedrooms in our new bungalow. Their children at this time are aged like this: Ricky seventeen years, Carolyn sixteen, Peta thirteen, Hannah eight, and Beth five years. I have to share my bedroom with one of them and to save disappointment they take turns to sleep in the next bed to mine. Brian and Julia squabble as to which of them should sleep in the double bed, so they, too, take turns, but they write it down on paper to make sure they know whose turn it is.

On Mothering Sunday of 1982 Michael and I went up to Brighouse to the christening of my last grandchild, Richard and Eirene's little Elizabeth Mary, generally called Beth. We spent a very happy day getting to know many of the friends they had made up north. Richard's school friend Andrew Speechley was there. He and his family have settled only a few miles from Richard's home. I enjoyed meeting Andrew again. Years ago when he was a teenager he helped me every Saturday on my egg-stall and was a great help and comfort to me after losing Sid. His wife, who is a professional cook, had made everything for the meal, and my, didn't it show! Their huge old oak refectory table was a picture, laden with the most gorgeous food. A whole fresh salmon sat in the middle of the table, surrounded by all its accessories. The trifles, cakes, and pastries looked so good. It was a very enjoyable occasion.

Now Richard has moved to Ripponden, Sidney to Bromyard, and Brian to Hull to work as a nurse, so I have only two of my children and three of my grandchildren in the village. But the others visit me often. David and Catherine were here last Christmas and Ingrid came to see me last summer, and these visits led to several family gatherings.

Epilogue

THIS fourth book of memories finishes when my age is 79 years, but I shall continue writing about happenings in my life and in this village of Wymeswold. The result will be more like a diary, but my grandchildren and later their children will learn just what happened right to the end of my working life or, to be more correct, to the end of my being able to write these things. Since I finished writing "Never Too Late", many more never-too-late happenings have taken place. I have been a special guest on Gloria Hunniford's programme on B.B.C.2 and the first person to be asked by the Leicestershire Oral History Archive to record tapes on village life from the early 1900s to World War II, a project sponsored by Radio Leicester and funded by Manpower Services. I have also been honoured by being asked to take part in the History Fair, organised by the Museum of Technology, to be held in Leicester in May 1986. The participating counties are Derbyshire, Leicestershire and Rutland, Lincolnshire, Northamptonshire and Nottinghamshire. My books, including this one, will be on show along with other local history books. I am also enjoying addressing meetings at ladies' clubs, book clubs, and Women's Institutes, so it seems never too late to start new enterprises.

I realize how lucky I am to enjoy such good health, when nearing the 80 mark, and to have such a wonderful family and friends who have helped in so many ways, so I will end by thanking them and my readers for the great happiness these books have brought me.

Other titles in the
Ulverscroft Large Print Series:

TO FIGHT THE WILD
Rod Ansell and Rachel Percy

Lost in uncharted Australian bush, Rod Ansell survived by hunting and trapping wild animals, improvising shelter and using all the bushman's skills he knew.

COROMANDEL
Pat Barr

India in the 1830s is a hot, uncomfortable place, where the East India Company still rules. Amelia and her new husband find themselves caught up in the animosities which seethe between the old order and the new.

THE SMALL PARTY
Lillian Beckwith

A frightening journey to safety begins for Ruth and her small party as their island is caught up in the dangers of armed insurrection.

THE WILDERNESS WALK
Sheila Bishop

Stifling unpleasant memories of a misbegotten romance in Cleave with Lord Francis Aubrey, Lavinia goes on holiday there with her sister. The two women are thrust into a romantic intrigue involving none other than Lord Francis.

THE RELUCTANT GUEST
Rosalind Brett

Ann Calvert went to spend a month on a South African farm with Theo Borland and his sister. They both proved to be different from her first idea of them, and there was Storr Peterson — the most disturbing man she had ever met.

ONE ENCHANTED SUMMER
Anne Tedlock Brooks

A tale of mystery and romance and a girl who found both during one enchanted summer.

CLOUD OVER MALVERTON
Nancy Buckingham

Dulcie soon realises that something is seriously wrong at Malverton, and when violence strikes she is horrified to find herself under suspicion of murder.

AFTER THOUGHTS
Max Bygraves

The Cockney entertainer tells stories of his East End childhood, of his RAF days, and his post-war showbusiness successes and friendships with fellow comedians.

MOONLIGHT
AND MARCH ROSES
D. Y. Cameron

Lynn's search to trace a missing girl takes her to Spain, where she meets Clive Hendon. While untangling the situation, she untangles her emotions and decides on her own future.

THE LISTERDALE MYSTERY
Agatha Christie

Twelve short stories ranging from the light-hearted to the macabre, diverse mysteries ingeniously and plausibly contrived and convincingly unravelled.

TO BE LOVED
Lynne Collins

Andrew married the woman he had always loved despite the knowledge that Sarah married him for reasons of her own. So much heartache could have been avoided if only he had known how vital it was to be loved.

ACCUSED NURSE
Jane Converse

Paula found herself accused of a crime which could cost her her job, her nurse's reputation, and even the man she loved, unless the truth came to light.

NURSE ALICE IN LOVE
Theresa Charles

Accepting the post of nurse to little Fernie Sherrod, Alice Everton could not guess at the romance, suspense and danger which lay ahead at the Sherrod's isolated estate.

POIROT INVESTIGATES
Agatha Christie

Two things bind these eleven stories together — the brilliance and uncanny skill of the diminutive Belgian detective, and the stupidity of his Watson-like partner, Captain Hastings.

LET LOOSE THE TIGERS
Josephine Cox

Queenie promised to find the long-lost son of the frail, elderly murderess, Hannah Jason. But her enquiries threatened to unlock the cage where crucial secrets had long been held captive.

A GREAT DELIVERANCE
Elizabeth George

Into the web of old houses and secrets of Keldale Valley comes Scotland Yard Inspector Thomas Lynley and his assistant to solve a particularly savage murder.

'E' IS FOR EVIDENCE
Sue Grafton

Kinsey Millhone was bogged down on a warehouse fire claim. It came as something of a shock when she was accused of being on the take. She'd been set up. Now she had a new client — herself.

A FAMILY OUTING IN AFRICA
Charles Hampton and Janie Hampton

A tale of a young family's journey through Central Africa by bus, train, river boat, lorry, wooden bicycle and foot.

THE TWILIGHT MAN
Frank Gruber

Jim Rand lives alone in the California desert awaiting death. Into his hermit existence comes a teenage girl who blows both his past and his brief future wide open.

DOG IN THE DARK
Gerald Hammond

Jim Cunningham breeds and trains gun dogs, and his antagonism towards the devotees of show spaniels earns him many enemies. So when one of them is found murdered, the police are on his doorstep within hours.

THE RED KNIGHT
Geoffrey Moxon

When he finds himself a pawn on the chessboard of international espionage with his family in constant danger, Guy Trent becomes embroiled in moves and countermoves which may mean life or death for Western scientists.

DEATH ON A
HOT SUMMER NIGHT
Anne Infante

Micky Douglas is either accident-prone or someone is trying to kill him. He finds himself caught in a desperate race to save his ex-wife and others from a ruthless gang.

HOLD DOWN A SHADOW
Geoffrey Jenkins

Maluti Rider, with the help of four of the world's most wanted men, is determined to destroy the Katse Dam and release a killer flood.

THAT NICE MISS SMITH
Nigel Morland

A reconstruction and reassessment of the trial in 1857 of Madeleine Smith, who was acquitted by a verdict of Not Proven of poisoning her lover, Emile L'Angelier.

THE PLEASURES OF AGE
Robert Morley

The author, British stage and screen star, now eighty, is enjoying the pleasures of age. He has drawn on his experiences to write this witty, entertaining and informative book.

THE VINEGAR SEED
Maureen Peters

The first book in a trilogy which follows the exploits of two sisters who leave Ireland in 1861 to seek their fortune in England.

A VERY PAROCHIAL MURDER
John Wainwright

A mugging in the genteel seaside town turned to murder when the victim died. Then the body of a young tearaway is washed ashore and Detective Inspector Lyle is determined that a second killing will not go unpunished.

CHATEAU OF FLOWERS
Margaret Rome

Alain, Comte de Treville needed a wife to look after him, and Fleur went into marriage on a business basis only, hoping that eventually he would come to trust and care for her.

CRISS-CROSS
Alan Scholefield

As her ex-husband had succeeded in kidnapping their young daughter once, Jane was determined to take her safely back to England. But all too soon Jane is caught up in a new web of intrigue.

DEAD BY MORNING
Dorothy Simpson

Leo Martindale's body was discovered outside the gates of his ancestral home. Is it, as Inspector Thanet begins to suspect, murder?

TIGER TIGER
Frank Ryan

A young man involved in drugs is found murdered. This is the first event which will draw Detective Inspector Sandy Woodings into a whirlpool of murder and deceit.

CAROLINE MINUSCULE
Andrew Taylor

Caroline Minuscule, a medieval script, is the first clue to the whereabouts of a cache of diamonds. The search becomes a deadly kind of fairy story in which several murders have an other-worldly quality.

LONG CHAIN OF DEATH
Sarah Wolf

During the Second World War four American teenagers from the same town join the Army together. Forty-two years later, the son of one of the soldiers realises that someone is systematically wiping out the families of the four men.